Probing into out-of-the way points of interest in the West has been both a vacation and an avocation of Jim Martin for many years. Formerly a prolific freelance writer, Jim recently joined the staff of OUTDOOR LIFE MAGAZINE as Field Editor for the 11 western states.

When not off gathering materials in this exciting territory, or busy at home at his desk, you are likely to find him exploring in the Feather River Country where, together with his wife, Tiger, and young son, Jim, he makes his home.

View of Lake Almanor.

GUIDEBOOK TO THE FEATHER RIVER COUNTRY

BY JIM MARTIN

WARD RITCHIE PRESS • LOS ANGELES

The book is dedicated to TIGER,
my wife, without whose soft purrings
and occasional growls this book would
never have been written

The material in this book is reviewed and updated
at each printing.

Second printing, 1973

CONTENTS

5

*Bucks Lake viewed from an observation point
above the south shore.*

I INTRODUCTION

Discovering the Feather River Country of Northern California has been an avocation of the adventuresome for more than a century and a half. The Spanish explorer, Luis Arguello, is the first white man of record to have entered the territory. Arguello led his party into the awesome river canyon in 1817 and christened it Rio de las Plumas because of the many wild bird feathers he observed.

A lucky gold strike at Bidwell Bar on the Middle Fork of the Feather River in 1848 triggered an invasion of fortune seeking argonauts. Their quest for precious *oro* covered much of the tributary network. News from the gold mines brought streams of emigrants westward. Mountain man Jim Beckwourth guided the first wagon train over the pass which now carries his name and into the Feather River country in 1851.

Outdoor recreation is a major attraction in the territory today. The vast expanses of conifer forests, the numerous lakes both large and small, and the many miles of flowing waters make the region a mecca for modern day explorers who seek the rich rewards this exciting land has to offer.

What is the Feather River Country? Where does it lie?

On a map, the region reaches from the city of Oroville at the mouth of the main river canyon east to Beckwourth Pass near the Lassen-Plumas county line. All three forks of the mighty Feather River are naturally included, as are their many tributaries. Taking advantage of a writer's prerogative, I have also mentioned a few places that while not being in the tributary network per se, are so closely tied to the land I feel they rightfully belong.

The opening of trout season always attracts a crowd.

I have never found an exact description of the region in proper metes and bounds. Nor have I been able to ascertain an accurate accounting of just how many acres, or even square miles the territory embraces. But is this really important? I do know from probing into many of its fascinating corners that the country is wide, wonderful, richly rewarding, and in some spots still rather wild. This guidebook will cover many of its highlights.

If so inclined, a modern-day motorist could enter the Feather River country on State Highway #70, and without exceeding the posted speed limit, or even having to pause for a stop sign, could easily cross the region in about three hours time. Granted, he could later claim to have driven through the territory. Yet, alas, he would only have seen a brief sample of the country. This is also true of those visitors, and even part-time or permanent residents, who for various reasons fail to take time to explore beyond the confines of their immediate neighborhoods.

To know the region takes time. To appreciate it fully takes even longer. That's what this book is all about . . . a guide written to better acquaint visitors with this colorful and historical corner of California. Yesteryear and today have both contributed to the discoveries that await in the Feather River country. From the past have been gathered historical data and precious memories that make modern explorations so meaningful. These pages will provide guidelines which reveal what was once here, and to alert you as to what can be expected today.

The format follows an old family tradition . . . the Sunday drive. This custom is a bit of nostalgia my wife, son and I continue to enjoy. Individual chapters are written to cover a portion of the country that can be visited during a single day's drive. Should you elect to take longer, say to perhaps remain for a day or two, no one will deny you this pleasure.

Countless attractive campsites are available.

Seasons and weather conditions are important factors to consider when planning trips into the Feather River country. Many portions of the territory become snow bound during winter. Roads frequently are impassable in times of inclement weather. Knowing motorists never venture forth in winter without being properly equipped for driving on snow and ice. Snow tires, chains and anti-freeze are musts.

During summer many of the back country roads are dusty, rutted and used by monstrous logging trucks. Timid drivers in bright, new passenger vehicles may understandably choose to avoid them.

Major portions of the region are federal lands, and consequently open to public access. Sections of both the Lassen and Plumas National Forests embrace the territory. Maps of the forest districts can be obtained at any local ranger station or by writing the Forest Headquarters. For information about the Lassen National Forest, write Forest Supervisor, 707 Nevada Street, Susanville, Calif. 96130. Details concerning the Plumas can be obtained from Forest Supervisor, 500 Lawrence Street, Quincy, Calif. 95971.

Numerous attractive campground areas in both forests make the region a popular summer playground. Campfire permits are required in most campsite zones and can be obtained from any ranger station.

Carry, also, appropriate equipment for your favorite types of outdoor recreation. Angling, boating, exploring . . . hunting, rockhounding, bottle collection and wildlife photography . . . the region abounds in rich opportunities for high adventure. Which explains why those of us who know and love the land possess such strong feelings of affection towards the Feather River country.

The Feather River Fish Hatchery offers a close look at modern fish management.

II OROVILLE—CITY OF GOLD

The western gateway to the Feather River Canyon country, Oroville offers a delightful blend of the old and the new. It's a progressive modern community that is well attuned to the desires of today's travelers. The city is also a jumping off point for high adventures both near and far.

Much of the area's appeal lies in its close links with the golden past. Big news always seemed to be breaking around early day Oroville.

First came the discovery of gold in 1849 when a group of Argonauts heading for the strike at Bidwell Bar found rich colors along the river near the present location of the Feather River Fish Hatchery. A lively gold camp christened Ophir quickly blossomed on the site. The name Oroville wasn't adopted until 1855 when a post office was established. By 1856, the city had grown to become the 5th most populous in the state.

The quest for gold led the miners to the slopes of nearby mountains. A rich strike in Oregon Gulch focused attention on quartz mining. Hydraulic operations at Cherokee on Table Mountain produced both gold and diamonds. Activity reached its peak in this area during the 1880's.

In the 1890's action shifted back to the Feather River proper where a fleet of mammoth gold dredges was constructed to sift the gravels for paydirt. Giant mounds of rocks along the river today are testimony of their work.

Gold mining no longer plays a paramount role in the local economy, however vestiges of those spirited early times provide

13

fascinating rewards for Twentieth Century Argonauts who carry cameras instead of gold pans.

Several nostalgic points of interest can be visited by taking the designated sight seeing route through the city. A green center line and appropriate signs mark this pathway into the past.

CHINESE TEMPLE

An ornate Chinese temple on Broderick Street near the river levee is one of the most prominent landmarks on the Golden Feather city tour. Erected in 1863, the temple served as a religious, social and business center for the estimated 10,000 Chinese living in the area at the time. Dedication ceremonies for the house of worship were attended by representatives dispatched by the Emperor of China, who sent along a two ton brass incense burner for the "Temple beside the river."

As the number of Chinese residents dwindled over the years, the temple played a less important role until it was eventually abandoned. The city assumed title to the property in 1935 and restoration efforts were initiated. Today, the temple and the adjoining tapestry hall house one of the most impressive collections of Chinese art and artifacts in the nation. The facilities are open daily except on Wednesdays and Thursdays. A small admission fee is collected.

JUDGE LOTT HOME

Insight into the fashionable side of life in early day Oroville can be gained by a visit to the classic Judge Lott home in Sank Park on Montgomery Drive. Completed in 1856, just in time for the Christmas celebration, the stately dwelling served as the residence of Judge C. F. Lott and his family until bequeathed to the city by the Judge's son-in-law, Jesse Sank, as a memorial to

14

The Pioneer Museum.

his wife, Cornelia. The home and gardens encompass an entire city block. Visitors are welcome.

PIONEER RELIC BUILDING

Memories of early Butte County are carefully preserved in the County Memorial Museum at 2316 Montgomery Street in downtown Oroville. Situated on the site of the first sawmill in old Ophir, the rock walled building is maintained through the joint efforts of the Native Daughters and the Native Sons of the Golden West. Exhibits include a restoration of a black smith shop, carpenter shop, and a collection of pioneer artifacts said to be one of the finest in Northern California. The museum is open on Sunday afternoons and by special arrangement.

BEDROCK PARK

Bedrock Park, on the south bank of the Feather River, is a restful spot where visitors can pause to relax and perhaps ponder over the past. A shady picnic area and natural swimming pool make this a popular summertime retreat. Railroad buffs will enjoy a visit to Hewitt Park, off Baldwin Avenue, where a vintage steam locomotive is on display.

FEATHER RIVER HATCHERY

An impressive addition to the green line sight-seer's route, the Feather River Hatchery was constructed to compensate for salmon and steelhead spawning areas cut off by the Oroville Dam. The $3.2 million installation, one of the most modern fish hatcheries in the world, is designed to accommodate more than 11,000 adult salmon and steelhead spawners and has the capacity to handle 18 million salmon eggs plus 3.5 million steelhead eggs.

The tour route through the facility provides a close look into the operation of an up-to-date fish hatchery. Perhaps the most popular vantage point of all is the glass walled viewing chamber constructed into the fish ladder leading to the holding tanks.

Visitor activity peaks during the spawning run periods. Spring running king salmon generally commence arriving in June. The fall salmon run occurs from September to November. Steelhead spawners arrive during September, October and November, with a smaller run reaching the hatchery in spring.

AT REST IN PEACE

Of special interest to historians are the Pioneer Memorial Cemetery off Cherokee Road, which contains graves relocated during the construction of Oroville Reservoir, and the Jewish Cemetery located between Feather River Blvd. and the Freeway.

Although not his final resting place, a bronze plaque on a stone monument off Oro Dam Boulevard east of the city marks the site where Ishi, the last of the untamed Yahi Indians, surrendered himself into the custody of the whiteman in 1911. The intriguing tale of how this proud warrior managed to hold out until past the turn of the century is told in Theodora Kroeger's *Ishi, In Two Worlds,* published by the University of California Press.

Downtown Cherokee is a drowsy place.

III THE GOLDEN FRINGE

Oroville's colorful outback is a rich territory for exploration. Ghostly diggings from the mining days, inspirational spots of natural beauty, rewarding waters for outdoorsmen; all can be found within a short drive of the city limits. A network of secondary county roads provides easy access into the pastoral countryside, a region ripe with an exquisite rural flavor. During springtime, the hills and fields blaze with wildflowers. Red holly berries add a festive spirit to the winter scene.

The Cherokee Road which branches off Table Mountain Boulevard (the old Oroville-Chico highway) a short distance beyond the fish hatchery makes a good starting point. It's an easy-to-follow route that is little used by tourists.

A short distance after leaving the old highway, you will reach the turnoff to the Pioneer Cemetery which contains graves relocated during the creation of Oroville Reservoir. Deeper into the hills comes Oregon Gulch Road, a byway leading to the former mining camp called Oregon City. Little tangible evidence remains of this once busy supply center which today is marked only by a stone monument.

CHEROKEE

Almost, but not quite, a ghost town. This modest description of the faded hamlet on Table Mountain hardly does justice to the bustling community that thrived here during the 1880's. Yet even this may be considered an overstatement by some who visit the spot today.

Cherokee was reportedly settled in the 1850's by a New

Feather Falls is a photographer's favorite.

England school master, Sol Potter, who led a band of Cherokee Indians west from Oklahoma in search of gold. The town was named in honor of their tribal home.

Mining efforts in the dry hills proved rather bleak until the discovery was made that a stream of water played against a hillside would unlock rich gravels. Thus was born "hydraulicking," the mining process that would eventually rip away entire mountains and fill deep rivers with debris.

During the heyday of Cherokee more than 100 miles of flumes, ditches and pipes were constructed to provide water for the powerful monitor canons. The network, said to have cost in excess of $750,000, furnished 40 million gallons of water daily for the mountain sluicing nozzles. Millions in gold were extracted along with more than 200 precious diamonds.

The extensive hydraulic operations were so impressive, mining engineers traveled from near and far to marvel at the process. Among the notables that inspected the scene was President Rutherford B. Hayes.

Legislation restricting hydraulic mining eventually brought a halt to operations at Cherokee, and the town went to sleep shortly after. Slow healing scars on the mountain sides, tumbled walls, neatly lettered signs which explain their meaning, and a strong feeling of yesteryear mark the site today. From Cherokee it is only a short hop northward to State Highway 70 and a fast return to Oroville.

FEATHER FALLS

Feather Falls, one of the highest waterfalls in the nation, is among the highlights found along Oroville's Golden Fringe. The 640 foot plume on Fall River, a tributary to the Middle Fork, is the featured attraction of the Feather Falls Scenic Area. The

15,000 acre tract was set aside in 1965 to preserve its primordial splendor. The area also embraces a portion of the Feather River's Middle Fork, now a wild river.

You will have to hike in order to view the falls. A three mile foot trail leads from the designated parking area to the overlook point. Wear proper footgear and allow a minimum of five hours for the round trip. The falls are most spectacular in late spring and early summer when the melting snows of winter cause Fall River to flow at a peak level.

To reach the trail head, take Lumpkin Road east from Oroville to the town of Feather Falls, then follow Bryant Ravine Road to the parking area. Feather Falls, the community, was established in 1855 as a supply point for miners. Originally called Mooretown, the name was changed in 1937 when a lumber mill was constructed here. Milling operations shut down in 1970 and much of the population moved elsewhere.

THE BORROW PITS

Some good must come from every deed, a wise man once proclaimed. Although the gold dredge operators who ravaged the Feather River to bed rock during earlier days had no way of knowing it, those countless heaps of rocks and the potholes they gouged out are now a rewarding playground for outdoorsmen and their families.

Blanketing a sizeable tract of bottomlands southwest of Oroville, the Borrow Pits area is a wilderness tangle of rocks, trees, vines and other vegetation. Numerous ponds of varying sizes add to the jungle atmosphere. The name, by the way, alludes to the tons and tons of rocks and gravel that were borrowed from here during the construction of Oroville Dam.

Today the state owns much of the Pits, which are maintained

as a wildlife area by the Department of Fish and Game. Bass, catfish and panfish are found in many of the ponds. Experienced anglers enjoy excellent sport on a year around basis.

Don't expect to find anything fancy when you plan a visit. A network of dusty, bumpy roads laces through the area. Otherwise, it remains unimproved. Access can be gained off West Oro-Dam Boulevard.

View of Oroville Dam and Lake.

IV THE LAKE OROVILLE COMPLEX

Superlatives become much in style when describing the Oroville Dam complex. The massive earthfill barrier, the sprawling 15,500 surface acre reservoir behind, the exciting outdoor playgrounds they provide . . . everything about this big water in the deep gorge measures on a grandiose scale.

The Visitor's Information Center and overlook point on Kelly Ridge is an excellent place to become better acquainted with the Lake Oroville story. Here you will learn impressive facts and figures about the dam which has been praised as a wonder of the modern world. The area lies at the east end of the dam and can be reached via Oro-Dam Boulevard. From time to time, tours through the dam and powerhouse installation are offered.

King-sized, also, are the opportunities for outdoor enjoyment found at the reservoir. For a first hand look at what's available, let's plan an armchair cruise along the one hundred and sixty-seven mile long scenic lake perimeter. The Spillway Marina on the opposite side of the dam is an ideal launching point, so let's go a-cruising!

The Spillway Marina, with its thirteen lane boat ramp, spacious paved parking lot, and picnic area is one of several facilities comprising the Lake Oroville State Recreation Area. All are either maintained or under the jurisdiction of the California Department of Parks and Recreation which charges normal, state-approved fees for their use. A lake map and fee schedule can be obtained from the area headquarters, 400 Glen Drive, Oroville, Calif. 95965.

On the first leg of our show-me cruise, we'll probe the North

25

Largemouth bass are abundant.

Fork Arm. Heading out from the marina, we'll keep the lake shore to our port side enroute.

Once past the first point of land, we enter Potter Ravine, one of the many excellent angling areas to be encountered along the shoreline. The ravine is one of numerous inlets in which trees and vegetation were left standing when the lake filled in order to provide cover for gamefish. These brushy areas all afford excellent habitat for largemouth bass.

From Potter Ravine we cruise northward to enter the narrowed canyon of the Feather River's North Fork. To starboard lies Forman Point, another popular angling area.

Continuing into the canyon we are now passing over a portion of the original Feather River Highway. Motorists who remember the narrow, winding road will recall the stretch as being one of the most scenic portions of the highway up the canyon.

Soon comes the Bloomer Primitive Area, one of several lake shore campground areas constructed for the exclusive use of boat owners. Facilities are primitive, but the feeling of seclusion is superb. A similar boat camping zone awaits directly across the lake, as does a smaller campsite area ahead at Goat Ranch.

A short distance beyond we encounter the confluence of the West Branch and the North Fork Arms. The remains on the hillside at this noteworthy junction mark the penstock which once led to the Big Bend Powerhouse. Built in 1908 as the first hydroelectric installation in the North Fork Canyon, the historic generator building now lies beneath the waves.

Turning to port we pass beneath the West Branch Bridge, an interesting double-decked structure carrying both State Highway 70 and tracks of the Western Pacific Railroad across the lake. The marina installation which appears next is a part of the Lime Saddle Recreation Area, a concessionaire operated facility that

Cruising the North Fork.

is popular with residents of nearby Paradise and Chico. Several choice stretches of angling water are located further up the West Branch Arm.

Reversing course, but still hugging the shoreline to the left, we enter Dark Canyon, an area formerly cut by old Highway 40 Alternate, as the Feather River route was once designated. The pavement can be seen leading into the lake at the head of the canyon. Then it's back into the main North Fork Canyon a long, looping course deep into the steep walled gorge.

On the left lies Big Bend Mountain in the Lassen National Forest. To starboard is a portion of the Plumas. Both tracts of national forest land retain the wild flavor of a territory touched only lightly by man. Enroute we pass several small tributary waters which trickle into the lake. The inlet at French Creek has been set aside for overnight use by self-contained houseboats.

The canyon walls narrow closer past French Creek. Lookouts should keep a sharp watch to starboard for signs of former railroad activity. The original railroad installation ran through here and older maps still show such whistle stop names as Blinzig, New Blinzig, David and Isaiah. Little tangible evidence of those early railroading days remains except some concrete foundations and the old rail bed.

A low, concrete dam, once used to divert water to the Big Bend Powerhouse marks the head of navigation up the North Fork Arm. It's an interesting spot for a swim, picnic, or perhaps an hour or so of fishing.

After retracing our route to the main body of the reservoir, let's continue our cruise. We can set forth from the Spillway Marina or from the Loafer Creek area in Bidwell Bar Canyon which lies off the Oroville-Quincy Highway. The latter area is popular with over-night visitors because of the excellent Class A campground found here.

Let's first set a course for the new Bidwell Bar Bridge which can easily be spotted to the east. Erected to replace the historic overpass which originally carried this name, the 627 foot high structure is said to be the tallest suspension bridge in the nation. Little evidence of this distinction is apparent during times of highwater, however, for most of the foundations are submerged.

Once under the bridge, the helmsman has two choices. To port lies the Middle Fork Arm; to starboard is the South Fork area. Let's investigate the former first; it's probably the wildest portion of the entire undeveloped lake perimeter.

Before the reservoir was created, the primitive beauty of the Middle Fork Canyon was known to few persons. The going up the roadless canyon was so tough that only the most adventuresome knew the rewards to be found here. Today, you can easily marvel at the rugged mountainsides, the fjord-like walls and the densely forested hillsides from the deck of a pleasure craft. Yet the magical wilderness aura remains much the same as always.

High above the headwaters scene rises Bald Rock Dome, a gargantuan granite outcropping which stands sentinel over this wild-river outpost. To the right of Bald Rock cascades the watery plume of Feather Falls. Swimming and fishing are popular in the lake itself, and the cove at Kanaka Creek is a favorite rendezvous of houseboaters.

Craig Saddle, located where the Middle and South Fork Arms join, is a popular cruising center for boaters wishing to use both portions of the lake. Anglers and waterskiers find it convenient for a day's outing. Campground space is available ashore for overnight visitors. Thanks to the protective mountains which shield the South Fork, the waters here are often calm when waves whip other portions of the lake.

FUN AT THE FOREBAYS

Born with the building of the dam, a pair of shallow forebays north of Oroville are integral parts of the State Recreation Area complex. Their primary function is as holding basins for a unique operation which pumps water back into the main reservoir for re-circulation through the powerhouse. A secondary mission is family fun.

The three hundred-acre Thermalito Forebay North, located just off the freeway, offers picnic facilities, a swimming beach, and maneuvering room for non-power driven pleasure craft. It's a great spot for sailboats.

The South Forebay is best known as a boating and angling water. Power craft are welcome here. Launching ramps are available at both forebays.

Not to be overlooked for its recreational possibilities is the 2,000 acre Thermalito Afterbay at the west end of Oro Dam Boulevard. The large, shallow waters offers year around angling and waterfowl hunting in season.

*The railroad tracks and the highway play leapfrog
through the Feather River Canyon.*

V HIGHWAY INTO THE CANYON

August, 1937, marked a time for high celebration in the Feather River country. After 70 long years of dreaming and 9 years of arduous labor, builders had succeeded in pushing a highway through the Feather River Canyon.

A gala banquet and ball in Oroville on the night of Friday the 13th touched off the festivities. The official dedication rituals came on Saturday at Grizzly Dome, a giant granite monolith in the North Fork Canyon. The event was climaxed by solemn ceremonial rites during which Governor Merriam and other dignitaries shared a peace pipe with Chief Winnemucca, tribal leader of the Paiute Indians.

A luncheon in Quincy, the Plumas County seat, and a joyous banquet in Reno Saturday night capped the dedication day ceremonies. On Sunday, a wild west rodeo was held in Portola to wind up the jubilee. Yes, folks had a reason for riotous revelry.

The three-day fete heralded completion of a 70 mile long stretch of highway linking Oroville with Keddie, seven miles north of Quincy. Constructed at a cost in excess of $7 million, the $100,000-a-mile highway gave local residents a direct, all-year road to the upper Sacramento Valley. The new road was designated State sign route 24, and was praised as a miracle of highway construction. Now numbered as State Highway 70, the highway is still considered one of the most scenic roadways in California.

It's impossible to travel the entire original highway today. The portion of the road from Oroville Dam to Jarbo Pass has been replaced by an alternate route. Much of the former roadbed has

When he couldn't go around a granite bluff, man turned mole to push his highway up the Feather River Canyon.

34

been inundated by waters of Oroville Reservoir. So let's take the shorter, quicker new route.

From Oroville it's a fast freeway to Wicks Corner, about six miles north of the city limits. Then it's a gentle uphill climb through rolling foothills to the reservoir. Enroute, you will pass side roads leading to Paradise, Magalia, Pentz, Oregon City and the Lime Saddle Recreation Area on the West Branch Arm of the lake.

An interesting double decked bridge takes both the highway and the Western Pacific railroad tracks across Oroville Reservoir. Like the original road, the train tracks also had to be rerouted when the lake was created. A rest stop and view point are located at the east end of the bridge.

After leaving the rest stop, the highway climbs sharply towards its crest at Jarbo Gap (elevation 2,330 feet). Three miles beyond the bridge is an observation point from which visitors can obtain a panoramic view of the upper valley and the coastal range beyond.

A chain warning sign at the Jarbo Gap Summit reminds motorists that snows can be expected in the mountains which lie ahead at any time during the winter months. Drivers are also cautioned to keep alert for rocks and deer on the highway.

After crossing the summit, the highway descends a long, gentle grade towards Pulga on the North Fork of the Feather. Several turn outs offer vantage points from which to view the deep gorge. Pulga means flea in Spanish, which gives credence to the thought that some early explorer may have been so plagued on the spot.

A pair of large suspension bridges remind visitors that railroad tracks also follow the Feather River Canyon through the mountains. Completed in 1909, the rails came first and naturally took the most advantageous route available. Because it was impractical to construct the highway on the same side of the river

Scenes in the old Rich Bar.

as the train tracks, the two routes play leap frog all the way up the canyon. Consequently where the train tracks bridge the canyon from south to north at the Pulga Crossing, the highway does exactly the opposite. This trend will be noted at numerous points in the canyon.

Past Pulga the highway runs close to the river for several miles, and soon passes the Poe Power Dam, one of several Pacific Gas and Electric Company hydro-electric installations found along the North Fork. Constructed without benefit of fish ladders, the power company dams have transformed the river from a one-time prime fishery to a series of sluggish reservoirs primarily populated by suckers, Sacramento pike and other rough fish. Only a few old timers can still give first hand accountings of those glorious days when majestic steelhead, giant salmon and trophy trout swam in the North Fork.

The Cresta Powerhouse comes next and about 3 miles beyond is a roadside rest area. Overnight camping is not allowed, but you are welcome to pause and picnic. Then it's through Arch Rock Tunnel, the first of three massive passages punched through solid granite walls when man was forced to turn mole in his efforts to conquer the canyon. Grizzly Dome Tunnel is next, after which comes Elephant Butte Tunnel, the longest of the trio.

The highway crosses the river near the mouth of Rock Creek and in quick succession come the Rock Creek Power House, the Bucks Creek Power House, and Storrie, a PG&E company town. It's back to the south bank of the river and on to Tobin Resort where the train tracks and the roadway again use twin bridges to reverse positions.

Tobin, named after a Vice President of the Western Pacific Railroad, is one of several resorts which prospered in the canyon before the building of the highway, when sportsmen rode "Fishermen's Special" excursion trains to enjoy the prime angling in the

Modern prospectors at work in the North Fork.

river. When the Cresta and Rock Creek powerhouses were built in the late 1940's, Tobin came to life as a headquarters for construction workers. The resort had a population of around 2,000 persons and had a reputation as being the largest liquor account in Northern California at the time.

Next comes the Injun Jim Campground, one of numerous US Forest Service facilities which dot the Feather River region. Hookup facilities are not provided, however separate zones have been set aside for tent campers and recreational vehicle owners. Campsites are seldom filled to capacity. The campground, and the small school located nearby, take their names after Jim Lee, an Indian who reportedly had a garden near this site.

Continuing onward, the road climbs a grade to the Rock Creek Dam and Reservoir. Several tempting trout streams flow into the canyon from the mountains to the left of the highway. A small sign near the head of the reservoir denotes the location of a natural soda water spring. A trail leading to the mountain lake country west of Ben Lomond Peak heads near the Maple Leaf Inn, formerly known as Guys Resort.

Memories of early gold rush areas are preserved at the Eby Stamp Mill, a feature attraction at the PG& E rest stop where Yellow Creek joins the North Fork. The heavy stamps were originally used in the White Lily mine near Seneca. Across the river lies the Belden resort and another USFS campground. The site is named after Susan Belden, a pioneer homesteader.

A mile past Belden, Highway 70 and the main North Fork of the Feather reach a parting. The side road to the left follows the North Fork up Caribou and into the territory covered in Chapter 12—*Below the Dam*. Our route continues up the East Branch of the North Fork to the Junction of Indian and Spanish creeks.

The highway climbs sharply along the north side of the East

Branch, affording motorists an impressive view of the canyon-lands around Rich Bar, a vintage gold town so vividly described in Dame Shirley's *Letters from the California Mines*, written in 1851 and 52. Now published as *The Shirley Letters,* the book provides fascinating insight into the life in an early California gold mining community. The site has been designated as a California Historical Monument, however warning signs remind visitors that the town is privately owned.

Whistle stops and watering places are important names in the Canyon. And so we pass Virgilia, Jack's Place, and the hamlet of Twain. Just shy of the latter, a side road leads to another of Smokey Bear's campsite areas.

Beyond Twain lies Grays Flat, where a large scale lumber mill once operated. Some milling is still done here, but the operation is by no means as extensive as when the Flat was the terminus of a five-and-a-tenth-mile tram line across the mountains capable of delivering a bundle of logs every three minutes.

The Feather River Hot Spring and Paxton come next. The former is one of several natural spas in the region; Paxton was built as headquarters for the Indian Valley Railroad. Once called Soda Bar, the town was renamed in honor of Elmer Paxton who helped construct the IVRR.

A well signed intersection marks the Greenville "Y" where Highway 70 joins with Highway 89. The latter route leads to the left and will be covered in Chapter 8. Continuing to the right, Highway 70 climbs to cross Spanish Creek, then proceeds to Keddie, the eastern terminus of the $7 million highway. Quincy, only seven miles ahead, will be covered in the next chapter.

VI QUINCY AND THE AMERICAN VALLEY

An impressive courthouse building in the center of town reminds visitors that Quincy serves as government headquarters for Plumas County. It's a distinction that dates back to 1854 when legislation was passed creating Plumas from a portion of Butte County.

The Act directed that a temporary county seat be located in American Valley until such time as voters could decide on a permanent site. A hotel owned by H. J. Bradley, one of the three commissioners named to organize the county, was so selected.

A townsite was laid out on a portion of Bradley's American Ranch and named Quincy after the city in Illinois from which he had emigrated to California. That fall, following a heated election race, Quincy managed to beat out rivals O'Neills Flat and Elizabethtown for the coveted title of county seat. A shake room behind the American Hotel served as the county's first courtroom. A State Historical Monument now marks the site.

Quincy soon blossomed as the economic and social center for the American Valley. A post office was opened in 1855. Numerous commercial buildings were erected.

Unfortunately, Fate did not treat the new city too kindly. A series of disastrous fires, starting with a major blaze in 1861, served to wipe out many of the original structures. Reconstruction efforts followed, yet with each conflagration disappeared a precious portion of pioneer Plumas County.

One of the many magnificent edifices wiped out by flames was the Plumas House, built in 1853. The handsome structure, said to be one of the finest hotels in the mountains, was destroyed in

The county courthouse in Quincy.

1923. The site has been designated a state historical monument and is so marked. The Quincy Hotel, successor to the Plumas House, was similarly destroyed in 1966. As of this writing it has not been rebuilt.

Touches of the old and the new grace Quincy today. Although modern store fronts and buildings are crowding out vestiges of the past, memories of yesteryears are preserved in some of the older, private residences which continue to add dignity to the community. The Stella Fay Miller home at 500 Jackson Street (opposite the courthouse) now serves as the county museum headquarters for the County Chamber of Commerce.

The Peppard Cabin on the Plumas Fair Grounds in East Quincy is another old time dwelling that has withstood the passage of time. The shake roofed log cabin was built in the 1880's by William Peppard on his homestead in Peppard Valley. In 1952 the cabin was moved to the fairgrounds where it serves as a pioneer museum.

Old Number 8, a 1907 Baldwin Steam locomotive is another fairground attraction that is popular with shutterbugs and steam railway fans. The 2-6-2 Prairie type engine is the pride and joy of the Feather River Shortline Railroad, a group of iron horse addicts, who placed it on permanent display.

The county fairgrounds are billed as being the "cleanest and greenest in the West." During the summer growing season the area is radiant with multi-hued petunias. Fair time, held each August, is perhaps the "biggest event" on the local social calendar. A featured attraction is the Pacific Coast Logger Championships, during which modern lumber jacks match wood skills for fame and fortune.

PIONEER SCHOOL HOUSE

By 1857, the population of American Valley had swelled to

*Old Engine No. 8 is on permanent display
at the fairgrounds in Quincy.*

assume small community status, and the need for suitable educational facilities was apparent. Quincy was considered too distant for easy commuting, so it was decided to build a school in the valley.

A sum of $375 was raised by popular subscription, lumber and manpower donated, and the first school house in Plumas County was erected.

On July 2, 1857, the newly elected trustees named S. A. Ballou as teacher at a salary of $60 per month. Nineteen freshly scrubbed faces reported for the first class session. It was a record figure in an era when other tasks for children took precedence over book learning.

In 1880 the Pioneer School was rated as superior in pupil accomplishment. The curriculum consisted of Latin, French, the sciences, higher mathematics, literature, and business principles; all taught by George Houghton. The school term lasted for ten months; six of which were the regular public school, the rest being financed by direct contributions of the proud parents.

The original building, although remodeled and moved to a new foundation, was still serving as a classroom when its centennial birthday was celebrated. The school house is now on display at the county fairgrounds.

ELIZABETHTOWN

Elizabethtown, or "Bettsyburg" as it was often called traces its title to the knightly spirits of early gold miners who saw fit to christen their newly born diggings on the edge of American Valley in tribute to Miss Elizabeth Stark, daughter of a civic leader, and the town's only unmarried woman. First called Tate's Ravine for Alexander and Frank Tate who found gold in a tree dotted gully two and a half miles from the present site of Quincy, Elizabethtown ripened and died between 1852 and 1858.

45

Life was short, sweet and apparently bountiful, for it was written that "the early settlers propped doors open with chunks of gold, and that children used nuggets for toys." This claim is somewhat dubious, but there is no question of the town's being prosperous.

School classes were initiated in 1854, a year which saw business licenses issued for three grocery stores, three merchandise marts, a butcher shop, bowling alley, and four bars. Also of record were two hotels, a Masonic temple, and a division of the Sons of Temperance. Lewis Stark, Betsy's father, served as postmaster and Justice of the Peace. This same year the miners saw their adored Elizabeth claimed in marriage when Judge Stark presided over the marriage of his daughter to Warren Blakesley.

An intense rivalry between Elizabethtown and Quincy climaxed in 1855 when the postoffice was moved to the latter community. It is not known which hurt the most—the loss of their postoffice or the marriage of Betsy; but from this time on the town quickly faded. No traces of the original buildings remain today, however a stone monument marks the townsite.

Modern Quincy is well suited as a headquarters from which to embark upon trips into the surrounding areas. Campers and recreational vehicle owners will find a county campground in East Quincy, adjacent to the Fairgrounds. Picnic facilities and a nature trail await at Gansner Park. Campgrounds and fishing for bass and catfish are available at Snake Lake and Smith Lake located northwest of the city.

VII EASTWARD OVER THE MOUNTAINS

East from Quincy, the Feather River Highway enters a recreational heartland of small towns, modern resorts, and a land with roots reaching deep into yesteryear. Historians know the territory as part of the original Quartz Township, one of two such territories so created when Plumas was carved from Butte County in 1851. The title alludes to the rich deposits of quartz gold discovered on Eureka Peak, or Gold Mountain as it was called at the time.

Modern Highway 70 from Quincy to Beckwourth Pass near the Nevada state line will probably seem tame to anyone who has just traversed the lower North Fork Canyon. Realigned and widened during the 1960's, the roadway is high-speed all the way. Yet for those who choose to linger and probe into byways, adventures aplenty are awaiting.

Just over the hill from East Quincy lies Thompson Valley, one of several scenic meadowlands to be found along the highway. To the right branches the historic Quincy-La Porte road discussed in Chapter 15. This is the turnoff we will be using. Greenhorn Creek is soon bridged, after which comes Chandler Road, a meandering country lane leading into the American Valley and known as the back route to Quincy. It's well worth investigating.

A modern roadside rest at Massack serves as a popular tourist stop. Restrooms and picnic tables are provided. At the top of the grade lies a giant circular section of rails known as the Williams Loop, a name of significance to railroad buffs. Christened after the engineer who designed it, the Loop is a unique circle with a nine-tenths mile radius so laid out to enable the roadbed

47

The Masonic temple in Beckwourth.

to maintain its one per cent grade. Patient shutterbugs may be able to catch a long freight train with cars on both tracks.

Spring Garden, named for the numerous freshwater springs found nearby, sleeps peacefully just off the main highway, and perhaps dreams of busier times. During the 1930's, the town was the southern terminal of an aerial tramway crossing over the mountains to Walkermine in the north. Noteworthy also, is the 7,343 foot long Spring Garden railroad tunnel which links the North and Middle Fork drainages of the Feather River.

Crossing over the summit, Highway 70 enters Long Valley and the Middle Fork Country. Sloat, a small town named in honor of Commodore John Sloat who raised the American flag over Monterey in 1846, lies about a mile off the highway on the banks of the river. Sloat was born as a flagstop with the building of the railroad. Today, lumbering is a mainstay of the economy, the first sawmill having been built in 1915.

Cromberg, originally known as Twenty Mile House, is a vintage hamlet that started in the 1880's as a trading post for miners and a stopover on the Reno-Quincy stage line. A Forest Service campground is located at the east end of Long Valley just beyond the Mt. Tomba Inn.

Blairsden, named for James Blair who played a key role in the financing of the Western Pacific Railroad, is closely linked with vacation life in Plumas County. Several resorts and lodges make the area a lively holiday hub during the summer season.

The famous Feather River Inn is now a private school and no longer serves guests. The golf course, however, is open to the public.

Sightseeing prospects are excellent around Blairsden, including the vintage hamlet of Mohawk, historic Johnsville, the Plumas-Eureka State Park, and the alpine lakes in the Jamison Basin. South on State Highway 89 lies Graeagle, a former lumber

Another view of the Masonic temple in Beckwourth.

town now developed as a summer home area. Graeagle is a gateway to the Lakes Basin Country.

Leaving Blairsden, Highway 70 swings away from the river and thus misses the whistlestop of Clio, another of the territory's pioneer villages. The original postoffice established in 1870 was called Wash, after the name of an early day resident. The present name was adopted in 1905 and is said to have been inspired by a pot-bellied stove bearing this tradename.

Beyond Clio is a promising territory for bottle hunters and relic searchers. During the 1900's, the town of Clairville was in full swing here with a lively assortment of dwellings and commercial establishments. It was a railroad boom town that quickly blossomed and died. The site is located about 2 miles west of Delliker and can be reached via USFS roads.

Delliker, back on the main highway, is a former lumber town that flourished during the early 1900's. The old buildings are rapidly being claimed by Father Time. A modern trailer park and subdivision continue to breathe life into the area.

Portola claims the distinction of being the only incorporated city in Plumas County. It's a community that is tied closely to the railroading history of the Feather River Country, having been served by three lines . . . the Boca and Loyalton RR; the Nevada, California and Oregon RR, and now the Western Pacific.

Records reveal folks had a hard time deciding what to call the young community. During its infant days, when the town was a logging camp, it was called "Headquarters" because it served in this capacity for the railroad builders. Between 1906 and 1908 the settlement was at varying times called Mormon, Imola, and Reposa. In time the postoffice department approved the present title, Portola.

Railroad continues to play an important part in the life of the community. Outdoor recreation is also coming on strongly. Portola is a jumping off point for Lake Davis and the national forest lands to the north. A county campground and picnic area is situated near the eastern city limits.

SIERRA VALLEY

Blanketing more than 200,000 acres in the headwaters country of the Feather River's Middle Fork is Sierra Valley, the "cow country" of Plumas County. The area was once called Beckwourth's Valley in honor of mountainman Jim Beckwourth who in 1851 discovered the pass which bears his name. At one time Beckwourth operated a trading post here.

The town of Beckwourth, although christened in tribute to the famous guide, was apparently not a part of his trading post operation. Beckwourth grew to fame as a railhead for the Boca and Loyalton RR, and an important shipping point for stage lines. From here wagons and coaches departed for Indian Valley via Notson Place, Flournoy Ranch, and Genesee. Back road explorers can still follow this historic route through Red Clover Valley. The road is now maintained by the Forest Service.

Speculation surrounds the reason why Vinton was named, however records indicate the original town was formed in the late 1890's as a railroad station called Cleveland. Later it was renamed Vinton. A post office was established on the site in 1897, together with a hotel and bar. From Vinton, state highway 49 leads south to Loyalton and Sierraville.

Chilcoot, the easternmost community in Plumas County, lies a short distance from Beckwourth Pass. One version states the town was named in honor of the famous Alaskan pass near Skagway. Others disclaim this theory and state the name is derived from the Indian word, Chilecatha.

The original townsite stood along the railroad tracks near the entrance to the tunnel leading through the Diamond Mountains

52

to Long Valley. At the time the spot was known as Summit. When the highway was built in 1936 Chilcoot was moved to the present location. From here it is only a hoot and a holler over the hills through Beckwourth Pass then on to Hallelujah Junction on US 395. Before leaving the territory, however, ghost town aficionados may wish to linger and search along the tracks for the remains of Rag Town. The site is about midway between Chilcoot and Vinton.

Fishing at Lake Bidwell is a family adventure.

VIII INVITATION TO INDIAN VALLEY

The Greenville Y, marking the junction of highways 70 and 89, is the starting point for a travel adventure into scenic Indian Valley in north central Plumas County. The territory has always held a fascination for explorers.

Discovery of the valley by the whiteman dates back to the Gold Rush era and the travels of Peter Lassen. Lassen and a companion, Isadore Meyerwitz, spent the summer of 1851 in the mountain meadowland and christened it Cache Valley. The following summer, Lassen returned to open a trading post at the north-east corner of the valley. Fresh vegetables were a specialty. A historical marker now stands on the site.

That same year, members of the Noble Emigrant party passed through the territory and called it Indian Valley because of the numerous Maidus living in the area. The former name soon lost favor.

Settlers followed to cultivate the fertile fields. Some of the ranchlands remain in the families of the original settlers. Many of the century old houses and out buildings are still in use.

The first few miles of highway 89 upstream from the Greenville Y parallel Indian Creek and run along the roadbed of the former Indian Valley Railroad, a seventeen mile long track which linked Paxton on the Western Pacific RR with the copper mining operations at Englemine. The first stop on the line was at Indian Falls, a townsite laid out around 1910. The Indian Falls Hotel enjoyed a good reputation for fine foods and hospitality and was a popular rendezvous for railroad travelers. There's not

A mill-stone marker stands on the site of the first permanent residence in Taylorsville.

much to see at Indian Falls nowadays, however some deep pools in the creek below are favorite swimming holes during summer.

A bustling gold mining venture before the turn of the century; a busy lumber town today—that's the story of Crescent Mills. Now silent are such prominent mines as the Crescent, Green Mountain, and Jackson, but memories of the millions taken from their depths are recorded in history. Economic activity at Crescent Mills currently centers around a sawmill and molding plant.

Greenville, the largest community in Indian Valley was christened in 1862 by patrons of a log cabin boarding house operated by Mrs. Green, the first whitewoman to reside in the area. Extensive gold mining operations in the mountains west of town gave impetus for its growth.

Round Valley Reservoir (also called Lake Bidwell) at the head of North Canyon was created to provide water for the mining activity. Several gold camps were located around its shores; however it would take a bit of searching to locate the remains.

Outdoor recreation is the attraction at the reservoir today. Good angling for largemouth bass, bluegill and catfish can be enjoyed on a year-around basis. Ice fishing is popular during winter. Campground facilities are available at the lake, but swimming and water contact sports are prohibited because the reservoir is a source of domestic water.

Families who enjoy camping will also find a public campsite area on Wolf Creek, just north of Greenville. A short distance further up the highway at the former Setzer Camp, a USFS road takes off to the right to climb Keddie Ridge. A self-guiding nature trail has been constructed part way up the mountain. At the top of the ridge, a logging road provides access to tiny Homer Lake, a natural trout pond nestling just under a high granite ridge.

Eastward from Greenville, a paved county road takes off to circle Indian Valley. The pastoral byway runs past the Green-

Ice angling is popular during winter months.

ville Rancheria, the Indian Mission, Peter Lassen Marker, then around Keddie Point and on up the North Arm. Many of the ranches observed enroute are those settled over a century ago.

At the head of the North Arm, the road enters Lights Creek Canyon and continues towards Englemine, which is covered in the next chapter.

To complete the circle tour of Indian Valley, take the unpaved road which runs along the south side of the North Arm. Enroute you will pass Peters Ranch and Creek, the turnoff to Beardsley Grade and Foreman Ravine. The next stop is Taylorsville.

One of the initial pioneers to enter Indian Valley was Jobe T. Taylor, an enterprising emigrant from Illinois. Taylor was impressed with the site and recognized the need for a supply point to serve the newly settled ranches and nearby gold mines. In 1852, Taylor laid out the townsite which still bears his name.

Taylorsville grew to become an important commercial and social center. A variety of business establishments were opened including a sawmill and grist mill owned by Taylor. A millstone from the latter, said to have been the first flour mill in the Northwest, stands as a historical marker in front of the Taylorsville schoolhouse.

Taylorsville was an important stopover on the stage routes to the outside world. Perhaps the most notable were the lines through Red Clover to Beckwourth, thence on to Reno, and the Quincy-Taylorsville Road over Mt. Hough via China Grade. The latter route was constructed by Chinese laborers who also dug the mill race through town.

Mt. Hough on the south side of the valley is the site of a Forest Service Lookout, one of several such outposts manned in the Feather River Country during the fire season. Visitors are welcome at all of them. A small granite basin beneath the peak contains Crystal Lake, one of the fishing holes local anglers seldom choose to talk about. A day on the mountain can be an exciting adventure. Access can be gained from Taylorsville, however much better roads branch off from State Highway 70.

A free campground and picnic area awaits in Taylorsville just beyond the rodeo grounds. The annual Fourth of July celebration includes a colorful parade and a full day of riding and roping at the rodeo area.

Upstream from Taylorsville the road enters Genesee Valley, site of extensive dairying and copper mining operations commencing in the 1860's. By the 1880's, Genesee was considered important enough to have its own postoffice. Hosselkus Creek, which enters the valley from the north, takes its name from the wonderful 1,000 acre ranch of E. D. Hosselkus, a pioneer settler.

Past Genesee, a Forest Service road branches south to follow Little Grizzly Creek to Walkermine and Lake Davis. Don't try this one during bad weather. Just before reaching the Genesee mill, another secondary road leads southeast along the old stage route through Red Clover Valley to Beckwourth. It, too, is seasonal.

XI GHOSTS OF COPPER

A well-defined belt of copper extending through north central Plumas County provides an exciting meeting grounds for rock hounds, pebble pups, ghost town collectors and others who cherish the outdoors. While gold first drew fortune seekers to the Feather River Country, the discovery of rich copper deposits in later years touched off a second miners invasion, although admittedly of less magnitude. Few persons are acquainted with the colorful copper boom, yet its story is one of the most intriguing chapters in the saga of the territory.

ENGLEMINE

One of the most important of the copper towns in Plumas County was Englemine, located on the banks of Lights Creek above the North Arm of Indian Valley. The name is spelled in the singular, however in reality two separate and distinct settlements existed—Upper Camp on the slopes of China Gulch and Lower Camp, further down in the canyon proper.

Upper Camp, the older of the pair, traces back to the discovery of copper bearing ore in the 1880's by Henry Engle. Engle recognized the high quality of his find and staked a proper claim. At the same time, he realized that production would be costly due to transportation difficulties. The nearest railhead was miles away in the Feather River Canyon. Nor was the primitive wagon road leading to his new found copper claim suitable for heavy hauling. A limited quantity of the richest ore was carted out to a smelter, but at best this was only a small scale operation.

One of the few buildings still standing at Walkermine.

Hopes rose in 1911 with the construction of a 500 ton blast furnace designed to allow for on-the-spot ore reduction. Angry protests over the resulting fumes soon brought a halt to the plan.

Efforts persisted, and in 1915 mining history was made when a minerals flotation plant was placed into production. This was the first such facility in the United States to depend entirely on oil floatation for the reduction of copper sulfides.

Production soon increased, thanks to the new plant; however, transportation continued to be a problem. Sacks of concentrates were trucked away in tractor drawn wagon trains to Keddie for rail shipment to a smelter in Utah. Even so, the operators were determined to find a better system.

Mile shortening strides occurred in 1916 with the completion of the Indian Valley Railroad to connect the mine with the Western Pacific tracks at Paxton. The broad gauge line cost an estimated $500,000 to construct and proved a most welcome addition to the Indian Valley economy.

Electricity came to Englemine with the stringing of a 38 mile long powerline over the mountains from the Great Western Power Company generating station at Butt Valley. So arrived the golden years of Englemine.

Englemine was strictly a company town with its own post-office, stores, boarding house, bunkhouses, and cabins for men with families. A grade school was opened in 1916.

The completion of a $536,000 mill at Lower Camp in 1924 marked a highpoint of operations. Production figures for the period show an output exceeding $1.5 million in copper, together with $67,257 in silver and $32,536 in gold. The site encompassed a total of one hundred and eighty-one mining claims, covering 3,740 acres, plus an additional nine hundred acres reserved for timber, tailing piles, and right-of-way.

Rising operating expenses coupled with a drop in the price of

View of Walkermine during its active days.

copper commenced to cause problems during the 1930's. Operations were at first curtailed, then eventually halted. By 1935 the mines were shut down completely and many of the buildings dismantled and carted away.

Little remains of Englemine today. Evidence of this one-time copper giant is preserved in some concrete foundations on the mountainside, a few tumbled cabins tucked away in the forest, and a gargantuan pile of sand on the banks of Lights Creek below the old townsite. This marks the tailings pile and is considered as a first-rate playground by small fry visitors. Fretting mothers will find Lights Creek a convenient spot to wash up the young 'uns after play.

Some activity exists at the site at the time of this writing, but this is in conjunction with a small recovery operation started in the 1960's and is not a part of the original operation. Portions of the property are now posted against trespassing.

WALKERMINE

Youngest of the ghost towns hidden away in the Feather River Country is Walkermine on the southern slope of Mt. Ingalls. At one time this was the largest copper mining operation in California. Operations reached a peak during the 1930's. Records indicate copper valued in excess of $1 million was produced during 1931 alone.

More than 500 workers were employed at Walkermine during its heyday. Another company owned town, the community consisted of one hundred and thirty-two houses, four bachelor bunkhouses, plus over three dozen private residences. In addition the town had its own postoffice, hospital, stores, motion picture hall, and schools for both grade and high school students. Visitors inspecting the tumbled ruins today find it difficult to envision how a community of this magnitude could vanish in such a short time.

Mining operations were spread over a four hundred acre site located between Mt. Ingalls and Little Grizzly Creek. A nine-mile bucket tram was used to carry ore over the mountains to the railroad siding at Spring Garden. During the winter months, when deep snows blocked the access roads, the tram line was also used to transport personnel and supplies.

Little remains of Walkermine at the present time. Low copper prices forced a shutdown in 1932 and the employees moved else-where. Many of the buildings were also relocated at the same time.

Visitors can reach Walkermine via the Forest Service road connecting Lake Davis with Genesee Valley. Drivers not accustomed to mountain roadways may find the going a mite rough. During inclement weather the road will be closed as it is throughout the winter months.

X AROUND LAKE ALMANOR

Located in the shadow of lofty Lassen Peak, Lake Almanor is a matriarch of mountain waters. Created by the Great Western Power Company over a half century ago, then acquired as part of the Pacific Gas and Electric empire, Almanor is the largest lake in Plumas County. As typical of any proper lady of distinction, the giant reservoir possesses a rich, colorful history.

The original plan to create a hydro-electric development on the North Fork of the Feather River in Plumas County was envisioned by engineers of the Great Western Power Company, who recognized the broad mountain valley known as Big Meadows as an ideal site for a reservoir. Big Meadows, at the time, was famous for its dairying industry and as a summer retreat for families seeking relief from the valley heat. Several excellent resorts in the meadows catered to visitors who traveled over the western mountains for their holiday periods.

The construction project called for a dam of multiple arch design at a site in the North Fork Canyon directly below the Big Meadows area. Construction of the barrier was barely underway when excavators uncovered a thick seam of clay instead of the solid rock foundation expected. When word of the discovery reached the cities downstream in the Sacramento Valley, alarmed citizens demanded the project be stopped because it was unsafe and posed a flood threat to their communities.

Undaunted, the engineers selected a new site and construction resumed. But not without more trouble. Irked by the appearance of motor trucks rather than mule drawn wagons, local residents banded to complain that the noisy contraptions frightened

Trout and Kokanee salmon make a big splash on the Lake Almanor angling scene.

their animals, turned roads into rivers of dust, and prevented the normal flow of traffic. Petitions were circulated demanding that the operation of motor vehicles be prohibited during daylight hours.

Progress eventually proved victor, and in 1914 the dam was completed. A gala dedication ceremony followed during which the new reservoir was christened Lake Almanor, a title composed from the names of *AL*ice, *MA*rtha, and Elea*NOR* Earl, daughters of Guy C. Earl, a Great Western Power Company vice President.

In 1916 flashboards were installed along the crest of the spillway to increase the lake's storage capacity. Increased demands for power continued, and in 1927 the old dam was replaced by a larger structure. The new barrier stretched 1,200 feet from bank to bank and measured 1,350 feet thick at the base. The resulting reservoir necessitated the relocation of roads along the lake shore, several burial grounds, and the town of Prattville.

The postwar boom in California gave Lake Almanor a new lease on life. Modern roads and motor vehicles added extra hours and distances to holiday periods. A mushrooming population clamoring for more playground areas probed deeper into the mountains. Recreationists started discovering Lake Almanor in ever increasing numbers.

Lake Almanor's latest new look came in the 1960's when the Pacific Gas and Electric Company (PG&E) embarked upon another project to raise the dam and thus increase the lake storage. At the same time, hundreds of snags were removed from the lake bed, and the shoreline was cleared of vegetation to the 4,490 foot elevation, the reservoir's brim full mark. Campgrounds, picnic facilities and a swimming beach were created in conjunction with the project.

Today, Lake Almanor offers visitors an exciting blend of out-

The Hamilton Branch is a popular fishing stream.

door recreational activities, including fishing for both cold water and warm water gamefish, boating and camping along the conifer fringed shoreline. Let's make a circle of the lake and see the area first hand.

Canyondam, a tiny community on Highway 89 near the dam makes a convenient starting point. Canyondam was born with the building of the dam. Today, tourism contributes a large percentage to its livelihood.

Driving the west shore highway (State Highway 89), we soon arrive at the Canyondam Beach and picnic area, a popular playground during the warm days of summer. Continuing we cross the top of the dam to reach a large lake cove that is a favorite rendezvous with anglers and water skiers. A free public boat ramp lies on the tip of the point.

Rocky Point comes next. Here, camping facilities are maintained by PG&E, which charges a nominal fee for their use. A brief jog off the main highway via the old county road brings us to Prattville, one of the towns located in the Big Meadows area before the lake was created.

Prattville is named for Dr. Willard Pratt who operated a hotel on the site during the late 1860's. The lake front from here to the Almanor Inn a few miles down the road hums with resort activity during the summer vacation season. A spacious Forest Service campground is located just beyond the Almanor Inn. Past the campground, the old highway rejoins the new, and we continue towards the northwest. An impressive panorama of Lassen Peak lies ahead.

Soon comes the junction with State Highway 36. To the left lie the wonders of Lassen Volcanic National Park. Temptation may prove great, but let's continue on our original mission and turn right to Chester.

Named after a community of the same name in Vermont,

Chester is another of the towns found in Big Meadows before the lake was born. Logging and tourism play important roles here today. Visitors are invited to take a fascinating tour through the large, modern Collins Pine lumber mill. Permits may be obtained at the company office.

East from Chester, the highway crosses the north arm of Lake Almanor via a causeway, then ascends Johnson Grade on its way towards Susanville. A modern roadside rest lies at the top of the grade. Shortly beyond, we turn to the right off Highway 36 to continue along the east side of Lake Almanor.

A side road to the right leads to the Lake Almanor Peninsula and the area's newest community, Peninsula Village. The peninsula area contains some of the finest homes found in Plumas County.

Past the Peninsula turnoff, the old county road again branches right into the Big Spring Cove resort area. Then it's back to the main road and across the Hamilton Branch of the Feather River. Again, we turn to starboard and continue along Almanor's east shore. Several of the lake's newest resorts are situated here, plus a PG&E picnic grounds and observation point. The Canyondam junction lies just beyond, and the circle is completed.

XI ABOVE LAKE ALMANOR

To the north of Lake Almanor lies a fascinating hinterland of free flowing streams, hidden lakes, and vast expanses of ever-green timberlands. Stretching from the eastern end of Lassen Volcanic National Park to the Caribou Peak Wild Area, the region is comprised for the most part of national forest lands. A visit to the ranger station in Chester will fetch a complimentary map of the Lassen National Forest showing access roads marked by the USFS numerical system. With this handy guide to assist us, let's look at some of the points of interest which await.

UPPER FEATHER RIVER

The territory embraces the upper tributary network of the North Fork, an area deeply revered by trout fishermen. Yet to be harnessed by dam builders, the streams flow cold, clear and untamed. Angling is a top draw, both for heavy-weight rainbows and browns which move upstream from Lake Almanor to forage and spawn, and by the far less sophisticated catchables which are regularly stocked throughout the summer months.

There's good fishing to be found all along the North Fork from Lake Almanor to its headwaters. Thrilling trout action also awaits in the many feeder streams, including Rice, Benner, Louse, Last Chance and Warner creeks. All tributaries to the lake are governed by a special late spawning season, so check the Fish and Game regulation booklet for details. Anglers fishing the North Fork will find campsites at the Rice Creek and High Bridge campgrounds, a pair of USFS installations approxi-

A busy beaver leaves his mark.

mately five miles upriver from Chester. Another attractive camp-site area is at Domingo Springs, a few miles away.

WARNER VALLEY

Cutting through the scenic valley which shares its name, Warner Creek is one of the main tributaries entering the upper North Fork. Named after a pioneer trapper, the valley is bounded in the west by steep lava outcroppings known as the Warner Rims, and by 8,045-foot Mt. Harkness to the east.

Formed by the confluence of Hot Springs and Kings creeks, which head within the national park, Warner Creek offers excellent trout fishing during season. That portion within the historic Lee Ranch is closed to public access, however there's plenty of good trout water awaiting above and below the ranch. The Warner Creek Campground at the lower end of the valley is operated by the Forest Service.

The road through the valley is paved to within a half mile of the park boundary. Keep alert for wildlife as you drive.

LASSEN VOLCANIC NATIONAL PARK

Shortly after leaving the upper end of Warner Valley you enter one of the overlooked corners of the park. Open to the public only on a seasonal basis, the area becomes snowbound each winter. Just inside the boundary are a ranger station and campground.

A few miles farther at the end of the dirt road is the Drakesbad Resort. Purchased from private owners by the government in 1958, the long famous vacation retreat is operated by a park concessionaire.

Located on Hot Springs Creek, the resort takes its name from Edward Drake who settled here in the 1860's. The "bad" comes from the German term for bath or spa, and alludes to the many

The Domingo Springs Campground.

hot springs nearby. The Devils Kitchen, a short hike west of the resort, contains many of these thermal springs and mud pots.

South of the resort, and reached by a self-guiding nature trail, is Boiling Springs Lake, an unusual body that is held to a constant temperature around one hundred twenty-five degrees by steam rising through underground fissures. Numerous bubbling mudpots are located here as well. Visitors are cautioned to remain on designated trails when exploring the area.

From the lake, trails continue on to Terminal Geyser and Devils Kitchen. A brochure describing the nature trail is for sale at the parking lot at the start of the trail.

JUNIPER LAKE

A fork in the road just west of Chester marks the gateway to Juniper Lake and the eastern end of Lassen Volcanic National Park, a lightly visited area of hidden lakes and beautiful forest trails. Only a small percentage of park visitors ever explore here in the east.

From Chester the road is paved for five and one-half miles into the forest, after which it becomes rather bumpy and dusty. The first few miles are bordered by privately owned property, after which comes the Lassen National Forest. Benner Creek flows close by. Campsites are available in the Benner Creek Campground. Many deer are seen in the territory, for this is the summer range of the Tehama herd. Take caution, however, for firearms are not allowed inside the park boundary which comes next.

Continuing around the eastern flank of Mt. Harkness (elevation 8,039 feet), we approach Juniper Lake.

The largest of the many standing waters inside the national park, the lake was so christened because of the juniper trees growing along its shoreline. The species is considered rare in the park. A campground and ranger station are situated at the lake.

Past Juniper the road becomes even bumpier as it heads towards Horseshoe Lake, named because of its configuration. A sign suggests the road is best negotiated by four-wheel drive, however experienced back country drivers using standard motor vehicles generally have no trouble enroute. Another campground and ranger station are located at Horseshoe Lake. As is true of Juniper, they are only open during the summer months.

WILLOW LAKE

A unique lake near the headwaters of Willow Creek makes an interesting destination for motorists who don't mind driving a rough road to find an unusual fishing hole. The water is Willow Lake, a twenty-seven surface acre natural body that is characterized by large areas of floating sod which in some spots extend out for over one hundred feet from the shoreline. Often called "floating islands" the sod is composed of a thick tangle of soil, sticks, grass, weeds and other debris. This buoyant bog affords concealment for trout and green sunfish and offers an interesting place from which to cast.

Anglers who venture out on the "island" soon discover that it will slowly sink under the weight of a person. So unless you keep shifting position you are likely to wind up knee deep in water. The eerie sensation is sure to generate amusement.

Willow Creek lies west of Warner Valley and can be reached by USFS road 29N14, which branches off the Domingo Springs Road. Camping is allowed at the lake.

CARIBOU WILDERNESS

Hikers who enjoy the wonders of an unspoiled alpine terrain will find the Caribou Wilderness Area, which lies north of Lake

Almanor, a ripe region for exploration. Named for a prominent peak inside its borders, the area is a pint-sized primitive region which measures roughly ten miles long and five miles wide. Yet it's chock-a-block with gem lakes and lush stands of virgin timber. The solitude of the forest is assured, for no motor vehicles are allowed inside the area.

The area was established in 1932 and even today is known to relatively few visitors. Excellent fishing for rainbow and eastern brook trout can be found in many of the seventy-odd lakes which dot the region. Not all of the standing waters support fish life, by the way. Some of the area's most promising lakes are Beauty, Posey, Evelyn and the Hidden Lakes in the south; and Triangle, Twin, Turnaround, Eleanor, Jewel and Caribou Lakes in the north, to name but a few. A network of well marked trails provides access to them all.

Access to the southern half of the wilderness is via a series of logging roads leading to Heckle Ranch. The turnoff is from Highway 36 just past the Johnson Grade Rest area. Roads are often in bad shape due to weather conditions. From the east, the easiest approach is along the Susan River road to Silver Lake. The Silver Lake campground makes a convenient jumping off point for day long adventures.

Under present regulations, Forest Service permits are necessary to visit a wilderness area. Permits are available from the ranger station in Chester.

An isolated anchorage at Butt Lake.

XII BELOW THE DAM

Deep in the North Fork Gorge below Lake Almanor lies one of the frequently overlooked corners of the Feather River Country. It's the twenty plus miles of canyonlands between the dam and Gansner Bar on Highway 70.

Discovered during the gold rush bonanza days, the region was worked extensively by ambitious argonauts. Considerable wealth was taken from the North Fork operations. Today, the territory is the domain of anglers, hunters and others who relish the outdoor life. And although visitors find rich opportunities for adventure here, the numbers of persons who travel here is surprisingly few. If you cherish almost forgotten byways, and don't shy away from dusty, narrow roads, it's an area well worthy of investigation.

Unofficial capitol of the North Fork Country is Seneca, a sylvan hamlet tucked away deep below the damsite. The name Seneca is said to have been adopted from an Indian word meaning "beautiful scenery." The title is so appropriate, let's not question its veracity. Seneca radiates a feeling that not all vintage gold towns are dead . . . some are merely sleeping.

Originally called North Fork, the town once was a scene of lively action and boasted its own post office, hotel, school, store, and a sizeable population of miners and their families. As late as the early 1940's, Seneca bustled with mining activity. Then came World War II. The draft and the call for war workers in the cities caused the mines to shut down for the duration. High operating costs and the present "unrealistic price of gold" have preserved the status quo.

Remains of the former hotel at Seneca.

To reach Seneca, take the county road branching south from State Highway 89 just past Canyondam. It's paved for a short distance, then turns to dust, gravel and a downhill grade first-time drivers are not likely to forget.

You won't find much at Seneca, today. The former post office and general store with the colorful message "Gold Dust Exchanged" was destroyed by fire during the 1960's. Only rubble and a rock chimney remain of the once popular hotel. Beautiful downtown Seneca currently consists of a picturesque bar, a single gasoline pump, and a cluster of cabins serving summertime visitors. Still there are those who predict that Seneca will rise again.

All it takes will be a rise in gold prices, they will tell you.

Even today the diggings are not deserted. Small scale mining operations are still being carried on. Strong rumors maintain that there's much more than a mite of color being extracted from the mines. Local residents, it is said, often carry a poke sack of gold; but it is best not to start asking questions until you are known in the area. In the interim you can always find action casting for trout in the river.

Shunting gold talk aside for a moment, let's continue down-river. From Seneca the dirt road twists and winds along the North Fork rim to reach Butt Valley Reservoir. If you enjoy visiting off-the-beaten pathway freshwater playgrounds, this is a spot for you.

Butt Valley is named for Horace Butt, a miner who settled here in the 1850's. The lush meadows supported a prosperous dairying operation and in 1910 a hotel flourished on the scene. The land was then purchased by the Great Western Power Company which created the lake in 1926 as a hydro electric storage reservoir. Today it is owned by PG&E.

Water skiing in the snag-free portion of Butt Lake.

Formed long before the days of the multiple usage concept, the reservoir is characterized by the skeletal remains of trees which died after the valley was flooded. The old snags make fine housing projects for ospreys, Canada geese, and other wildlife "critters."

During the 1960's, in a compromise move designed to please both pleasure boaters and conservationists, PG&E removed the snags from a portion of the lake to make room for water skiers. Campground facilities and boat launching ramps were developed at the same time.

A more direct approach to Butt Valley Reservoir is via a dirt road branching off from State Highway 89 near Prattville.

Buckle your seatbelts, take a deep breath, for it's time to resume our down-river explorations. The steep grade below the Butt Valley dam is the downhill grade to Caribou. Flatlanders may consider the trip a bit scary, but take comfort; special charter sightseeing buses negotiate it periodically during PG&E "show me" tours.

Caribou was born in the gold rush era and was a lively camp at the time. Old timers preferred the spelling Cariboo, a name they associated with Canadian gold fame.

A PG&E power installation and collection of company residences and buildings at the foot of the grade mark modern Caribou. Started in 1919 by the Great Western Power Company, the Caribou powerhouse was placed on the line in 1921 as the second plant built by GWP. Old Caribou, the gold camp, was located down the canyon at Crablouse Ravine.

The original town had a reputation as a rip roaring settlement with a population estimated to number around one thousand. Hydraulic mining played a key role in the Cariboo operation. Water for the minitors was brought by flume from Butt Creek.

In later years, the power company rebuilt the flume to carry water for its turbines.

At Caribou the road again becomes paved and from here on it's smooth driving to Highway 70. Access to the river is easy at many points along the roadway. Fishing is generally good. Motorists wishing to remain in the area will find attractive campsites in the Queen Lily, North Fork and Gansner Bar campgrounds.

XIII THE HUMBUG-HUMBOLDT COUNTRY

Travel over the mountains between Big Meadows and the upper Sacramento Valley was a challenging adventure before the turn of the century. It still is today, if you choose to follow the same routes used by the pioneers. This chapter takes us along a pair of those early day wagon routes into the territory which lies west of Lake Almanor. On the first leg of the trip we will drive out of the Feather River Country via the historic Humbug Road. On the return we will cross the mountains on the old Humboldt Toll Road.

Allow a full day of traveling time for the round trip. While modern motor vehicles cover ground at a much faster gait than those clip-clopping buggies and buckboards of yesteryear, our mission will cover a much greater distance. Your map of the Lassen National Forest will be a great aid to navigation.

The starting point for the circle tour is Forest Service Road 27N11, which branches south from State Highway 89 on the west side of Lake Almanor. The turnoff is marked by a sign. Be sure to top off your gasoline tank before leaving the lake.

Approximately one-half mile into the forest the road forks. To the right is the Humboldt Road over which we will return. For the present, turn left on Road 27N01 leading to Longville and Stirling City. This is the Humbug Road.

Soon comes Butt Creek, one of the better trout streams in the area and a popular retreat for summer campers. Downstream lies Butt Valley Reservoir which was covered in Chapter 12.

Crossing a gentle ridge, we follow Miller Creek into the Humbug Valley and the site of old Longville. The vintage townsite,

Fine fishing awaits in the lakes south of the
Humbug summit.

of which little remains today, took its name from W. B. Long, who ran cattle in the valley during the mid-1850's.

A pleasant meadowlands threaded by Yellow Creek, Humbug Valley was settled in 1850 by an enterprising Bavarian emigrant, Andrew Miller. Chronicles are rather hazy as to exactly how the name "Humbug" was selected, although one version attempts to link it with "Crazy" Stoddard and his quest for legendary Gold Lake.

Andrew Miller was a busy man. He grazed a large herd of cattle in the lush fields, engaged in a bit of farming, and later erected a resort hotel near the point where we entered the valley. Miller also served as the local postmaster and as a Plumas County supervisor from 1862 to 1867. The Miller family still owns property in the valley, including a stately white house on the hillside near the road intersection.

A natural soda spring just off the Yellow Creek Road makes an interesting point for a rest pause. Indians valued the waters for medicinal purposes long before the whiteman settled the valley. Records maintained by the homesteaders praised the waters as a balm for stomach trouble. Some users find the bubbling waters highly refreshing.

The spring has been restored as a point of historic interest by the Pacific Gas and Electric Company, which also maintains a small campground not far away. Yellow Creek offers good trout fishing in season for catchable-sized rainbows, plus a population of more sophisticated browns. The area is popular with deer hunters in the fall.

An important link with the outside world, the old Humbug Road left the west end of the valley to cross over Humbug Summit, then drop into the Sacramento Valley via Stirling City and Magalia, or "Toad Town" as it was often called. Portions of the former roadway were marked by shingles nailed to trees. We

Even a log out into the water can make a good fishing spot.

won't spot any of these markers today, but the drive over the summit will recapture a bit of the old stage coach days flavor.

Leaving the valley, USFS 27N01 heads west past the Little Grizzly Ranger station and campgrounds towards the crest of the grade. Serious anglers may wish to side track towards Sunflower Flat to the south, then on to Green Island, Saucer and Frog lakes. Access is via logging roads, but you will have to complete the final leg by foot trail.

Crossing the Humbug Summit (elevation 6,714 feet) the road enters Butte County. From here it is a downgrade drive past Butte Creek House, Snag Lake, and the turnoff to Philbrook Reservoir where a Forest Service campground awaits.

Soon comes a time for decision. Ahead along the Humbug Road lie Inskip (where the pavement begins), Stirling City, Magalia, Paradise and Chico. To the right branches USFS 26N01, a direct route to Butte Meadows where we will commence our return trip via the Humboldt Road. Some motorists may wish to take the long way around and proceed on to Chico, then return to the mountains along State Highway 32 to Butte Meadows. Those who elect to shun the city can follow the more direct route.

HUMBOLDT TOLL ROAD

Known at various times as the Humboldt Wagon Road, the Idaho Road, and Major Bidwell's Road to Humboldt, the Humboldt Toll road was a controversial subject during the early 1860's, when rival interests debated as to the best route between Chico and Susanville. In 1863 the state legislature gave John Bidwell and a group of friends a franchise to operate a toll road between Chico and Honey Lake in Lassen County. The group incorporated as the Chico and Humboldt Wagon Road Company· and commenced building the roadway we will follow on our return to Lake Almanor.

Motorists who elect to go directly from the Humbug Road to Butte Meadows without visiting Chico will miss the first section of the old toll road, now State Highway 32. Early accountings describe it as being "winding and tortuous and so narrow in some spots that freight teams wore bells on the harness so that lighter outfits could hear them coming in time to find a place to turn out of the way." Way stops on the climb uphill from Chico included Hog Springs; 10 Mile House; 14 Mile House, with the Toll Gate just beyond; 16 Mile House, now called Forest Ranch; and Lomo, where State Highway 32 turns away from the old wagon road.

Butte Meadows, the initial stopping point after leaving Highway 32 was site of an early day hotel. A Ranger Station and campground are the most prominent features found here today. Three miles past the guard station, the road enters the Lassen National Forest. The Cherry Hill Campground is just inside the boundary. Two more miles and we reach the ghost town of Jonesville. Here the pavement ends. No longer in use, the historic Jonesville Hotel was still standing at the time of this writing. Visitors wishing to remain overnight may use the nearby Forest Service campsite area.

After a three and a half mile ascent, we crest at Humboldt Summit (elevation 6610 feet) to enter Plumas County, where the road narrows. Just over the ridge we come to Robbers Roost, so called because a masked highwayman once held up a passing stagecoach at the spot.

Descending the mountain slope, the road reaches Ruffa Ranch in the headwaters country of Butt Creek, which we crossed earlier in the day.

XIV THE OROVILLE-QUINCY ROAD

Before the completion of the highway up the North Fork Canyon in the 1930's, the most direct and important route between Oroville and Quincy was a narrow, unpaved byway that saw its origin as a trail for pack trains. Originating at Oroville, the route wound into the mountains via Bidwells Bar, Buck's Ranch, and Meadow Valley, then on to the county seat. With the passing of each mule string, the trail wore deeper until eventually it was improved to allow travel by wagon and stage coaches. The first stages to travel the complete route made the trip in 1858, according to one authority.

Much of the road improvement was performed by toll road operators during the transitional period from pack trains to wagons. In 1855, a toll road was built between Quincy and Spanish Ranch in Meadow Valley. The next year a toll road was pushed from Meadow Valley to Buckeye. A company was later formed to provide a toll service all the way from Oroville to Beckwourth Pass, but the project failed to get launched.

Deep snows during the winter severely hampered travel over the route. Attempts to overcome such difficulties included the use of dog teams and cleverly designed snow shoes for horses. Even today, snow banks block access over the old road during the winter months; but since Highway 70 is an all-year route, no attempt is made to keep the former route open. Snowmobile enthusiasts often make the trip from Meadow Valley to Bucks Lake. The rest of the way remains closed until late spring.

In this chapter we will re-trace the historic back road from Oroville over the mountain. Travel is not advised until after

Water skiing at Bucks Lake.

94

the snow packs are gone, say around the first of June. The route is designated USFS 24N25, and is indicated on a map of the Plumas National Forest. Copies may be obtained from the Headquarters Office in Quincy or at the Oroville Ranger Station.

From Oroville we head west to Lake Oroville and the new Bidwell Bar Suspension Bridge. Quincy lies less than 60 miles away, a distance we can easily cover in a few hours; yet a drive oldtimers regarded as an overnight trip.

After leaving Lake Oroville we climb slowly along Canyon Creek to the town of Berry Creek and Lake Madrone, where subdividers have been active. The road now commences to climb, and we soon pass Brush Creek and Mountain House, a popular stop for weary coach travelers and a pausing point even today. Not far beyond Mountain House the pavement ends, and we enter Plumas County.

Climbing steadily we reach Merrimac, one of the overnight stops on the old route. The Rogers Cow Camp Campground area is a half mile to the west. Then comes Elks Retreat and Buckeye, both towns in name only. Near here the stage coach was held up by Black Bart in 1878. The discarded express box was recovered and is now a proud possession of Plumas Parlor 219, NDGW. Other coach robberies were reported along the route, but no serious attempt was made to credit them to Black Bart.

As the road continues to climb, we can better appreciate the hardiness of those early coach drivers and their passengers. So it's on over Soapstone Hill and Grizzly Summit (elevation 5,788 feet), Frenchman Hill and a descent into Haskins Valley. A monument on the north side of the road marks the grave of P. Linthiough, who was buried here in 1852. The Pioneer Grave is registered historical landmark 212.

Wild geese beg a handout from a summer home resident.

A side road to the south leads to Grizzly Creek Forebay. Ahead lie the Grizzly Creek Campground and the turnoff to Lower Bucks Lake. If the spirit of adventure prevails, you may wish to detour to the lower lake, then on to Three Lakes, at the head of Milk Ranch Creek. The trio of isolated tarns provide water for the Bucks Creek Power House, and offer good fishing for brook trout.

We pick up the pavement shortly before crossing Haskins Creek at the east end of the valley. Soon comes a campground maintained by PG&E. Bucks Lake lies just ahead.

Bucks Ranch, now hidden under the waters of Bucks Lake, was named for Horace "Buck" Bucklin, who settled here in 1850. Bucklin did not remain in the mountain valley for long, but the ranch bearing his name grew and prospered as a cattle operation and an important stage stop on the Oroville-Quincy line. Any traveler who has just climbed over the summit will appreciate what a welcome spot the stage station must have been. During the peak of operations, Bucks Ranch had a hotel, store and post office, together with several ranch buildings. The hotel was destroyed by fire in January, 1928, the same year the lake was born.

Created by the Great Western Power Company as another hydro-electric water impoundment, Bucks Lake stretches three miles in length and measures from one to 2 and a half miles across. When full the surface covers 1,827 acres, and the scenic shoreline twists and winds for fourteen magical miles. The shores of the reservoir display a split personality. Summer homes and resorts ring the southern half. The northern perimeter retains its wilderness flavor, although this pristine status has long been eyed by timber cutters and developers.

Popular as a summer retreat for boat owners, campers and

anglers, Bucks Lake boasts a large and growing fan club. Because the reservoir supplies water for power generators, it is subject to severe drawdowns, especially during late fall before winter rains commence to collect. To see the lake at its photogenic best, schedule a late spring or early summer visit.

Continuing past the lake, the road reaches Whitehorse Campground on Bucks Creek. Just beyond we come to Bucks Summit. Then it's down, down, down past the former toll gate site and into Meadow Valley.

Meadow Valley, so named for its picturesque mountain setting, was the site of two of the oldest and most important settlements in pioneer Plumas County. The village carrying the name of the valley originated in 1851 when Wilson Dean erected a log cabin on the site as a trading post. A hotel, and store were built a year later. In time the town had a post office, sawmill, blacksmith shop, and several homes. A friendly rivalry existed between residents and those of Spanish Ranch, a couple of miles across the valley.

The name "Spanish Ranch" entered the pages of Plumas County history in 1850 when a pair of Mexican wranglers settled in Meadow Valley, where they initiated a business caring for pack animals belonging to the miners and raising cattle for the local market. A trading post was opened there in 1851. Other stores, saloons and three hotels were soon added, making the village an important supply center for outlying mines. A post office became a part of the community in 1858, and ten years later a Wells Fargo & Company express office went into operation to handle coin and bullion from the Monte Cristo mine on Spanish Creek. A Chinese community numbering several hundred came to settle along Silver Creek and re-work the diggings

98

left by the Mexican miners. Their two-story joss house was a showplace of the valley.

Not much evidence of those olden days remains in Meadow Valley today, although the community still has its own post office, several business establishments, together with many private residences, mostly built in recent years.

And the modern paved highway leading to Quincy is a far cry from the former horse and buggy toll road. It's too late to embark upon an extended angling adventure today, but take note of the forest roads leading south off the main road while driving to Quincy. They lead to the edge of the Middle Fork Canyon and some fabulous fishing, as will be discussed in Chapter 16.

Lake Delahanty was created to supply water for hydraulic monitors.

XV THE LA PORTE AND QUINCY WAGON ROAD

One of the earliest supply routes leading into the newly opened gold camps in the Feather River Country led from Marysville through Strawberry Valley to La Porte, then over the mountains to Onion Valley, Nelson Creek, and on to the American Valley. Originally only a pathway for pack trains, the trail developed through use and hard labor into a road suitable for wagon travel. The adventure we embark upon in this chapter takes us over this still but lightly used byway; and, with a bit of nostalgic reminiscing, back to those golden days.

The lower portion of the route was the first to assume status as a wagon road. The first stage operation occurred in 1851 when McElhany, Thomas and Company organized to provide service between Marysville and Onion Valley, a camp so named because of the numerous wild onions growing in the vicinity. Everts, Snell & Company initiated express service over the route that same year but apparently did not carry passengers. While stages reached Onion Valley, wagons did not commence rolling all the way to the American Valley until several years later.

The La Porte-Quincy road, which we plan to follow, was born in 1866 when the State Legislature, in some political maneuvering, authorized the building of such a road. Funding was another problem; however, the lawmakers gave local residents permission to vote on a $20,000 bond measure to finance construction. The proposal received voter approval during an unusual special election conducted in 1866.

La Porte carried the balloting with a landslide 467 ayes and nary a nay. Of special interest is the fact that when voters again

Ruins of old Gibsonville today.

assembled on the following election day only 175 persons turned out. The drop in number might indicate that many of the miners who strongly favored a wagon road had presumably moved elsewhere. Another version has it that the citizenry of La Porte was not against a bit of "politicking" themselves, including stuffing the ballot box. In any event, the road was eventually completed, so let's take a drive.

Invoking a writer's prerogative, I have selected La Porte as our starting point. You will cover many captivating miles while driving to this charming old gold town from Marysville, or other valley communities, however the territory below La Porte is in the Yuba River Country, which rightfully belongs in another volume.

The long and colorful history of La Porte first took shape in 1850 with the discovery of gold along Rabbit Creek at the head of Little Grass Valley. Excited Argonauts christened the spot Rabbit Diggings, a name which lingered for several years. By 1854, the village had grown to become a bustling mining camp with its own postoffice, hotel, stores, saloons and other enterprises, plus many cabins and houses. The economy boomed a year later with the introduction of hydraulic mining on a large scale. Scars carved by the giant monitors are readily apparent on the hillsides around town.

Feeling more sophisticated, the Rabbit Creekers were no longer content with the name of their town. In 1857 they selected the name La Porte, which was suggested by Frank Everts, a leading citizen who came west from La Porte, Indiana. The town continued to thrive, but not without problems. A series of serious conflagrations continued to raze the community almost as fast as the structures were rebuilt.

Prosperity reached a peak in La Porte during 1862, after

which a decline started. Yet the spirit to survive persisted. In 1866, following a vain attempt to become the seat of a new county to be called Alturas, La Porte was annexed to Plumas County. Authorization for the wagon road came as part of the legislative maneuverings leading to the boundary change.

Before we depart from La Porte, it is fitting to give recognition to the role this remote mountain settlement played in the history of American skiing. As deep snows came to block the trails, the miners met the situation by fastening "Norwegian snowshoes" to their feet which allowed for travel over the frozen crusts. The hand-fashioned runners were in reality a form of skis. A friendly rivalry quickly developed as to which men were the fastest skiers. Informal races were held which in time led to the formation of the Alturas Ski Club, which conducted downhill races for cash purses.

Today, La Porte claims the distinction of being the "birthplace of competitive skiing." Should you choose to pause to talk snow sports, you'll hear lots more about life in old La Porte. If you plan to remain overnight, a Forest Service campground on the outskirts of town makes a convenient spot to bivouac.

Beyond the campground, the pavement forks. To the left lies Little Grass Valley Reservoir, one of the new lakes in the territory, where campsites and recreational facilities are provided. The road we are following branches to the right. We lose the black topping soon after turning.

Ascending Gibsonville Ridge, the road reaches the tumbled remains of Gibsonville, one of several enchanting gold camps (Mt. Pleasant, Whiskey Diggins and Hepsidam) which flourished in the area during the 1850's. Diligent search yielded no clue as to why Hepsidam was named, however records reveal that Gibsonville was christened in honor of the prospector who first found paydirt on the site. Gibsonville grew rapidly and soon had several thousand residents. As late as the early 1900's, the town still thrived with two large hotels, a Wells Fargo Building, brewery, several stores and numerous private residents. Hydraulic mining helped keep business humming.

But you won't find much activity today. When laws shut down the giant nozzles, mining halted and many of the buildings were dismantled and moved away. Still, an assortment of KEEP OUT signs give warning that a lot of the old claims remain in private ownership.

At Gibsonville the road again forks. The branch leading to the northeast is the back road to Johnsville via Lake Delahunty and the headwaters of Nelson Creek. Lake Delahunty is a reservoir created in 1861 to provide water for the hydraulic monitors. Johnsville will be covered in Chapter 17.

Leaving Gibsonville, the old wagon road skirts Pilot Peak then drops into Onion Valley, another vintage gold camp now in ruins. Then it's along Washington Hill, across the Hog Back, and on to the brink of the Feather River's Middle Fork Canyon. Descending sharply we cross Nelson Creek and proceed to the townsite called Nelson Point.

Credit for opening this corner of the Feather River goes to a miner named Nelson, who had been attracted to the area by the rumors of "Crazy" Stoddard and his lake of gold. Nelson and a companion found paydirt in the creek which now carries his name. The news brought an invasion of hopefuls into the Middle Fork Country.

Gold camps blossomed everywhere. On Nelson Creek alone were such now all but forgotten camps as Graveyard Flat, Fiddler's Flat, Buckeye Flat, Henpeck Flat, Grizzly Flat, Scotch Flat, Meeker Flat, Independence Bar, Dixon Creek, Union

Creek, Poorman's Creek and Hopkins Creek. Modern maps often fail to designate exact locations, although creeks are sometimes depicted.

Nelson Point, the largest of the towns, was the most stable and possessed a hotel, boarding house, stores, saloons and several cabins. Even it now exists in name only.

Dropping to the river, the road crosses the Middle Fork of the Feather. This is one of the few spots where passenger vehicles can reach the remote canyon which has been given wild river status. The fascinations to be found deep in the gorge are covered in the next chapter.

Leaving the Middle Fork, the road becomes paved and continues through Thompson Valley to Highway 70. Quincy lies only a short distance away.

XVI THE WILD RIVER

Trout streams come a dime a dozen in the Feather River Country, yet if you were to ask any knowing local sportsman to name the best of the lot, nine times out of ten he will tell you: "the Middle Fork." The term will mean just one place, the rugged gorge where the Middle Fork of the Feather River flows wild and free onwards towards the sea. And although natives have never had a reputation for being loose lipped when it comes to revealing the locations of their favorite fishing holes, most folks talk freely about the Middle Fork. It's so inaccessible, angling pressures remain light.

Rated by many sportsmen and conservationists as being the finest natural trout stream remaining in California today, the Middle Fork Canyon offers prime opportunities to enjoy fishing for wild trout in a setting of spectacular natural beauty.

The tributary network of the Middle Fork drains a 1,240 square mile area encompassing portions of Plumas, Sierra and Butte counties. When speaking of the Middle Fork Canyon, however, most folks have in mind the river section between the whistle stop called Sloat and Lake Oroville more than 40 miles downstream.

Here runs an untamed river which has changed but little with the passing of time. Native Indians were the first to roam this wild, rugged land. Gold seekers opened the remote gorge for the whiteman, but they didn't remain long. Today Nature has reclaimed the canyon as an adventureland for the outdoorsman who seeks the rich rewards of a wilderness territory.

Steep walls ring both sides of the gorge, making access diffi-

*To best savor the splendor of the remote Middle Fork
gorge plan a hiking visit and a stay of several days.*

cult if not impossible at many points. Thick stands of timber and shrubbery are abundant. Ponderosa pine and fir predominate on the slopes of the upper river. Black oaks, live oaks, and California Bay are common in the lower zone. Alders, cottonwoods and willows line the riverbanks throughout the entire canyon. Wildlife is abundant with deer, bear and many varieties of small game finding sanctuary in the remote canyon.

The Middle Fork is a fast flowing river that drops steadily from an elevation of 3,700 feet at Nelson Point just off the La Porte-Quincy road down to 900 feet at Lake Oroville. The gradient of sixty-two feet per mile along the way makes for an abundance of deep pools interspersed with long riffles. Fishery biologists describe the river as excellent trout habitat.

The high quality trout fishing found in the wild canyon draws most visitors to the Middle Fork, but as indicated earlier the number of anglers is relatively few. Wild native rainbows are so plentiful it is often possible to hook and release dozens of prime fish during a single day's effort. Brown trout lurk here as well, and often reach trophy sizes. Squawfish, suckers and carp also dwell in the river pools, but since environmental conditions favor trout, the rough fish have not taken over.

Because of its inaccessibility, the river canyon is not heavily fished. Flies, lures and baits are all productive, however most anglers who seek trophy trout use worms, grasshoppers or hellgrammites which they work in the deeper holes. Water conditions play an important role in determining angling success. Fishing is generally poor during the periods of the spring runoff when the river is high and roily. This is not a particularly good water upon which to open trout season.

Roads into the canyon are few. Passenger vehicles are only able to reach the river at two points in the Wild River portion—

the crossing on the Quincy-La Porte road and at Milsap Bar many miles down river where a Forest Service road (USFS 21N12) leads down. The remote stretch in between is reserved for serious sportsmen willing to work in order to reach select fishing holes.

Numerous jeep trails and foot paths work their way down from the canyon rim. Trails average one and two-tenth per mile along the forty-five mile stretch of river from Nelson Point to the mouth of Fall River. Many of these access ways were originally hacked out of the steep walls by early day Argonauts. Tumbled shacks, abandoned mine shafts and relics from the gold era are to be found throughout the canyon. Sharp-eyed searchers may also discover vestiges of such former camps as Minerva Bar, Rich Bar, Hottentot Bar, Sailor Bar, Rocky Bar, Columbia Flat, Sunny Bar, Bray's Bar, Bowen's Bar, Frenchman's Bar, Willow Creek, Poverty Flat, Popular Bar, Peoria Bar and Nigger Bar—all names of note during former years.

To reap the maximum enjoyment from a visit, plan an overnight stay. Make it several days if possible. Suitable bivouac areas can be found on almost any sandbar or at the foot of the trails. Cool, fresh water is available from any number of springs. Almost every side ravine supports a tiny creek.

Trails are steep. While a fast moving hiker can easily reach the river in less than an hour, at least twice this amount of time should be allotted for the climb back out. The going up grade is tedious, especially for persons not accustomed to hiking. By all means, avoid making the ascent during the middle of the day when temperatures can be downright hot. Trails leading into the canyon are shown on the US Geological Service charts for the Blue Nose Mountain, Onion Valley, Bucks Lake, Cascade and Brush Creek quadrangles.

During the 1960's a question mark surrounded the Middle Fork as water developers cast envious eyes on the free flowing river. Today the future of its primordial splendor is apparently assured, thanks to the Wild and Scenic Rivers Act of 1968 which named the Middle Fork as a component of the national wild rivers system. Management of the 25,000 acre river area created was assigned to the Forest Service. Plans call for administering the river as three zones . . . a wild river, a scenic river, and a recreational river.

The Wild River portions include a five and four-tenths mile stretch from Lake Oroville upstream through Bald Rock Canyon, and a twenty-seven and 5-tenths mile long segment through Devil Canyon up to Nelson Creek. The Scenic River zones encompass a three and six-tenths mile long area at Milsap Bar, and a six and one-tenth mile portion from Nelson Creek to the Spring Garden railroad tunnel. The easily accessible area above the tunnel all the way to Sierra Valley has been classified as a Recreational River zone. Planning details for the entire system are available for public review at the office of the Regional Forester, 630 Sansome Street, San Francisco, Calif., and at the Plumas National Forest Headquarters in Quincy.

View of Jamison Lake.

XVII THE LAKES BASIN COUNTRY

The enchantments of a once rip-roaring mining town that steadfastly refuses to assume complete ghost town status, an impressive new addition to the California State Park system, and a charming alpine wilderness reserved for the enjoyment of hikers can all be found by turning south off the Feather River Highway near Blairsden. Our adventure target in this chapter is the scenic Lakes Basin Country and the adjoining Plumas-Eureka State Park. The region is a land of picture postcard mountain lakes, majestic cloud scratching peaks, and ripe golden memories.

Eureka Peak is perhaps the most famous of the granite crags which tower above the Sierran setting. Its steeply inclined slopes once rang with the sounds of hard rock miners who tunneled deep within its bowels for gold bearing quartz. The sagas of the Plumas-Eureka Mine, the Jamison Mine, and others are indelibly etched in the pages of Feather River history. Below the mines lay old Johnsville, Eureka Mills and nearby Jamison City, each a gold mining great in its own right. Time has stilled these once bustling communities and the extensive mining operations from which they drew their livelihood, yet precious memories of those golden years remain. Come, let's make a visit.

THE LAKES BASIN

The rewards of an alpine world are easy to claim in the Lakes Basin Recreation Area, a delightfully unspoiled mountain territory which straddles the Plumas-Sierra County line south of the Mohawk Valley. To savor these treasures fully, however, you must be willing to walk, as this is a hiker's haven. In order to

113

safeguard the region's delicate natural beauty, regulations have wisely been adopted which prohibit cross country vehicle travel.

These restrictions impose no hardships, for a network of easy-to-follow footpaths laces the region, and good roads lead to each trailhead. The Lakes Basin Campground, a USFS facility located just off the Gold Lake road which leads up from Graeagle, makes a convenient headquarters from which to commence explorations.

Of the many shanks-mare adventures awaiting in the basin area, one of our favorites is a loop tour leading out from the campground to cover several of the area's most interesting lakes. The circuit can easily be completed in a day with ample time allowed for angling, swimming, and sightseeing. So it's forward march.

Big Bear Lake comes first. It's just over the hill from the campsite area and offers fair to good fishing for rainbow trout. It also makes a refreshing swimming hole on a warm summer day, although somewhat nippy temperatures may curtail actual time spent in the water. The next stop along the trail is Little Bear Lake. In times of high water this appears to be an extension of its big brother. Here, too, you should be able to catch a rainbow or two.

The pathway continues on to Cub Lake where eastern brook trout provide a challenge. Because the waters are limpid and fairly shallow near the shore, anglers must cast far out to tempt a cautious trout.

Leaving Cub Lake, the trail rises rather abruptly to crest on a ridge above Long Lake, the second largest in the Lakes Basin group. Here the trail branches with the left hand fork leading to Mud, Hellgrammite and Silver Lakes—each well worth investigating.

Long Lake is a deep water that contains many large rainbow trout. Most visitors fish it from the shoreline, however some of the best catches are made while trolling from a boat. Resort operators occasionally have a craft or two on hand for hire, but you can't always count on one being available. A lightweight inflatable rubber boat will be a big help if you plan to spend any time angling at Long Lake. After leaving the lake, the trail descends rapidly on its return to the campground.

The circular route described is but one of several memorable outdoors adventures awaiting along the network of trails in the Lakes Basin area. Another popular hike-in is a visit to the lakes in the basin at the headwaters of Jamison Creek. Recommended access is via the trail leading up from the state park.

Four excellent lakes—Grass, Rock, Jamison and Wades—dot the Jamison Basin. During the golden era they supplied water for the mines. Today they offer fine fishing and an opportunity to camp under the stars. Because of heavy visitor use during recent years, carte blanche camping is no longer allowed anywhere in the recreation area. Regulations do allow overnight stays at the four lakes named as well as at Smith Lake. Information can be obtained at the Mohawk Ranger Station.

PLUMAS-EUREKA STATE PARK

Of the many gold mines opened in the Feather River region, none played a more prominent role than those on Eureka Peak. At first gold fever was slow in spreading to this portion of the territory. Some placer mining activity occurred along the banks of Jamison Creek as early as 1850; hard rock mining was reported in the following year. Yet at best, activity was only on a small scale until the 1870's when attention was turned to the quartz veins deep inside Eureka Peak. The catalyst came in

115

Main Street of Johnsville.

1872 when the Sierra Buttes Mining Company of England moved in to consolidate operations. This marked the start of boom times.

The story of that golden era in its authentic setting comes to light at the Plumas-Eureka State Park, one of the most recent additions to the California State Park system.

Established in 1959, the park grounds embrace over 5,000 acres of dramatic hardrock mining history, including a large portion of Eureka Peak, where over 70 miles of tunnels have been gophered into its granite core. The shafts and tunnels are considered too dangerous for visitors and are marked OFF LIMITS, but the above-ground areas are preserved and open to park users.

Valuable insight into those early mining days can be gained at the park museum, located in a former bunk house building. More memorabilia is on display outside.

A shutterbug's favorite is the partially restored Plumas-Eureka mill whose mighty stamps are credited with having crushed over $80 million in gold. Still standing as well is a portion of the tramway which once carried the ore to the crushers. Historians explain that the original tram line was the first ski lift in America. The story of the Alturas Ski Club and its competitive meets is related in the park museum.

Operated on a year around basis, the state park is an outstanding campsite area during the summer months. In addition to the historical points of interest, visitors will find good fishing waters closeby. Because campsite space is often at a premium, visitors may wish to take advantage of the reservation system. Details can be obtained by writing Plumas-Eureka State Park, Johnsville Star Route, Blairsden, Calif. 96103, or the Department of Parks and Recreation, Box 2390, Sacramento, Calif. 95811.

Winter time activity finds park visitors busy on the ski slopes, where an organized ski club offers family memberships at bargain rates. Members take turns operating the tows and snack bar in the warming hut.

Immediately outside the park boundary is Johnsville, so named for William Johns who served as superintendent of the Plumas Eureka mining operation. The community slumbers in contentment now, but its weather-worn houses and buildings tell of far more prosperous years. Photographers will find many challenges while strolling the streets of town. Visitors should keep in mind that this is not state property, and the structures are not open to the public.

XVIII NEW WATERS IN A TIME-HONORED LAND

Adding another reservoir to a territory already liberally dotted with lakes might easily pass unnoticed if not for the efforts of an aggressive press corps. Such is the case with the Upper Feather Project, a vital segment of California's gigantic State Water Plan, under which several new lakes were envisioned in the tributary network of the Feather River.

The outdoor recreational potential of the new waters was given a top billing when the project was being sold to the voters. Grandiose plans were unveiled showing the recreational benefits which would stem from the new mountain reservoirs.

Five waters were approved for the Upper Feather River Project. Antelope, Davis and Frenchman reservoirs have already been completed. Plans for two more—Abby Bridge and Dixie Refuge reservoirs—are still on the drawing boards at press time.

FRENCHMAN RESERVOIR

Frenchman Reservoir, the first of the Upper Feather River Project lakes to be created, started to fill in 1961 following the completion of a large rockfill dam on Little Last Chance Creek in eastern Plumas County. The creek is another of the landmarks with names that trace back to the wanderings of "Crazy" Stoddard. It is said that here is where Stoddard was given a final opportunity to lead his party of treasure seekers to the nugget strewn shores of Gold Lake.

The 1,580 surface lake itself is christened to commemorate

119

*Tributary inlets are productive fishing holes
at Frenchman Reservoir.*

Claude and Simon Seltier, brothers who settled in the area during the 1880's after emigrating from France. Situated ten miles north of Chilcoot on Highway 70, the reservoir lies in a mile-high valley ringed with grass and sage brush flecked hills. The conifer forest touches the lake shore in some spots. When at high level, the shore line stretches for twenty-one miles.

Frenchman Reservoir made angling history in the early 1960's as being the best trout water in the state, a distinction attributed to heavy plants of rainbows in the food-rich waters of the young lake. Angling continues to rank high with the action at a peak during spring and again in late fall. Bank casters do best along the shoreline near the dam and in the tributary inlets. Trollers enjoy good results working the off-shore waters.

Swimming and water skiing receive a big play during the summer months when water temperatures warm to a comfortable level. During winter the lake surface is often ice bound. Campground, picnic and boat launching facilities are located on the east side of the lake near the dam. Another campsite area lies in the canyon below the reservoir.

ANTELOPE RESERVOIR

Proponents of the State Water Plan proudly point out that Antelope Reservoir was created primarily as a recreation water, a role it is fulfilling in honorable style. Situated in a forest-fringed valley at the headwaters of Indian Creek, Antelope Lake covers nine hundred thirty acres when brim full. The shoreline stretches for thirteen miles, a distance which seems much longer because of the numerous inlets and coves. Pines, firs and cedars reach to the water in many locations.

Although the reservoir is among the youngest of the Feather River lakes, the scenic mountain valley for which it is named

Angling at Antelope Reservoir.

traces back to the pioneer days of Plumas County. Each year, after the snows left the region, stockmen drove cattle into the valley to fatten on the meadow grasses along Antelope, Boulder, Indian and other creeks. The lush pasturelands produced rich milk and prime beef. Records tell of heavy firkins of creamy butter being shipped regularly to markets in Virginia City and other areas where gourmet foods were in demand.

Fishing is a big draw at the lake where the degree of sucess depends primarily upon the current stocking program of the Department of Fish and Game. Rainbow trout are the most abundant species, however some large German browns are occasionally taken. The creek below the spillway is a popular spot each year when trout season opens due to the large number of fish concentrated in the area.

Trollers do well all over the lake. Recommended spots for short casters are along the face of the rock fill dam and in the inlet coves.

Campgrounds and a paved boat launching ramp are maintained by the Forest Service during the visitor season, which extends from spring through the first snows of winter. Once the storms arrive the lake surface freezes and access roads are blocked.

Antelope reservoir is most easily reached from Indian Valley. Take the county road through Taylorsville, then up through Genesee Valley. The pavement extends as far as the Genesee mill. More adventuresome drivers who enjoy back country exploration may choose to use the dirt Forest Service roads which lead in from the north and east. Do not attempt these routes during inclement weather.

LAKE DAVIS

Named in memory of Assemblyman Lester Davis, a veteran

legislator from Plumas County, Lake Davis lies in the National Forest lands north of Portola. Recreation, the enhancement of downstream fishing, and a source of domestic water are listed as its major objectives.

The reservoir is most noted for the trout fishing it provides. Like most new waters, the lake provided excellent angling during its fledgling years, with many large rainbows counted in creel checks. The present fishery is maintained by the Department of Fish and Game, however some natural reproduction occurs in the tributaries. Consult the angling regulations for opening dates on the streams.

Bank fishermen score well off the face of the dam and adjoining coves. Boat anglers enjoy good catches either trolling or still fishing with baits. Excellent fly fishing can be found by wading the shallows at the upper end of the lake. Angling reaches a peak during the evening hatch just before dusk.

Campgrounds and boat launching facilities are located on the north shore and are maintained by the Forest Service. The entire south shore is reserved for day use only. Three easy access roads lead in from Highway 70, however they are generally closed by snow during winter. The road along the north side of the lake continues on to Walker Mine and the Genesee Valley.

INDEX

126

127

$1.95 EACH—WESTERN TRAVEL & LEISURE BOOKS FROM THE WARD RITCHIE PRESS

Trips for the Day, Week-end or Longer
ALL BOOKS COMPLETE, MOST WITH PHOTOGRAPHS AND MAPS

QUANTITY

		TOTAL
☐	**BACKYARD TREASURE HUNTING**	$ _____
☐	**BAJA CALIFORNIA:** Vanished Missions, Lost Treasures, Strange Stories-True and Tall	$ _____
☐	**BICYCLE TOURING IN LOS ANGELES**	$ _____
☐	**EAT,** A Toothsome Tour of L.A.'s Specialty Restaurants	$ _____
☐	**EXPLORING BIG SUR, CARMEL AND MONTEREY**	$ _____
☐	**EXPLORING CALIFORNIA BYWAYS, #1** From Kings Canyon to the Mexican Border	$ _____
☐	**EXPLORING CALIFORNIA BYWAYS, #2** In and Around Los Angeles	$ _____
☐	**EXPLORING CALIFORNIA BYWAYS, #3** Desert Country	$ _____
☐	**EXPLORING CALIFORNIA BYWAYS, #4** Mountain Country	$ _____
☐	**EXPLORING CALIFORNIA BYWAYS, #5** Historic Sites of California	$ _____
☐	**EXPLORING CALIFORNIA BYWAYS, #6** Owens Valley	$ _____
☐	**EXPLORING CALIFORNIA BYWAYS, #7** An Historical Sketchbook	$ _____
☐	**EXPLORING CALIFORNIA FOLKLORE**	$ _____
☐	**EXPLORING SMALL TOWNS, No. 1**—Southern California	$ _____
☐	**EXPLORING SMALL TOWNS, No. 2**—Northern California	$ _____
☐	**EXPLORING THE UNSPOILED WEST, Vol. 1**	$ _____
☐	**EXPLORING THE UNSPOILED WEST, Vol. 2**	$ _____
☐	**FEET FIRST:** Walks through ten Los Angeles areas	$ _____
☐	**GREAT BIKE TOURS IN NORTHERN CALIFORNIA**	$ _____
☐	**GUIDEBOOK TO LOST WESTERN TREASURE**	$ _____
☐	**GUIDEBOOK TO THE DELTA COUNTRY OF CENTRAL CALIFORNIA**	$ _____
☐	**GUIDEBOOK TO THE COLORADO DESERT OF CALIFORNIA**	$ _____
☐	**GUIDEBOOK TO THE FEATHER RIVER COUNTRY**	$ _____
☐	**GUIDEBOOK TO THE LAKE TAHOE COUNTRY, Vol. I.** Echo Summit, Squaw Valley and the California Shore	$ _____
☐	**GUIDEBOOK TO THE LAKE TAHOE COUNTRY, Vol. II.** Alpine County, Donner-Truckee, and the Nevada Shore	$ _____
☐	**GUIDEBOOK TO LAS VEGAS**	$ _____

[SEE MORE BOOKS AND ORDER FORM ON OTHER SIDE]

☐	**GUIDEBOOK TO THE MOJAVE DESERT OF CALIFORNIA,** Vol. 1—The Western Mojave	$ _____
☐	**GUIDEBOOK TO THE MOJAVE DESERT OF CALIFORNIA,** Vol. 2—The Eastern, Includes Death Valley & Joshua Tree National Monuments	$ _____
☐	**GUIDEBOOK TO THE MOUNTAINS OF SAN DIEGO AND ORANGE COUNTIES**	$ _____
☐	**GUIDEBOOK TO THE NORTHERN CALIFORNIA COAST,** VOL. I. Highway 1	$ _____
☐	**GUIDEBOOK TO THE NORTHERN CALIFORNIA COAST,** VOL. II. Humboldt and Del Norte Counties	$ _____
☐	**GUIDEBOOK TO PUGET SOUND**	$ _____
☐	**GUIDEBOOK TO RURAL CALIFORNIA**	$ _____
☐	**GUIDEBOOK TO THE SAN BERNARDINO MOUNTAINS OF CALIFORNIA,** Including Lake Arrowhead and Big Bear	$ _____
☐	**GUIDEBOOK TO THE SAN GABRIEL MOUNTAINS OF CALIFORNIA**	$ _____
☐	**GUIDEBOOK TO THE SAN JACINTO MOUNTAINS OF CALIFORNIA**	$ _____
☐	**GUIDEBOOK TO SOUTHERN CALIFORNIA FOSSIL HUNTING**	$ _____
☐	**GUIDEBOOK TO THE SOUTHERN CALIFORNIA SALTWATER FISHING**	$ _____
☐	**GUIDEBOOK TO THE SOUTHERN SIERRA NEVADA,** Including Sequoia National Forest	$ _____
☐	**GUIDEBOOK TO VANCOUVER ISLAND**	$ _____
☐	**NATURE AND THE CAMPER.** A Guide to Safety and Enjoyment for Campers and Hikers in the West.	$ _____
☐	**TREES OF THE WEST:** Identified at a Glance.	$ _____
☐	**WHERE TO TAKE YOUR CHILDREN IN NEVADA**	$ _____
☐	**WHERE TO TAKE YOUR CHILDREN IN NORTHERN CALIFORNIA**	$ _____
☐	**WHERE TO TAKE YOUR CHILDREN IN SOUTHERN CALIFORNIA**	$ _____
☐	**WHERE TO TAKE YOUR GUESTS IN SOUTHERN CALIFORNIA**	$ _____
☐	**YOUR LEISURE TIME . . . HOW TO ENJOY IT**	$ _____

WARD RITCHIE PRESS
3044 Riverside Drive, Los Angeles, Calif. 90039

Please send me the Western Travel and Leisure Books I have checked.
I am enclosing $_____, (check or money order). Please include 25¢
per copy to cover mailing costs. California residents add state sales tax.

Name _____

Address _____

City _____State _____Zip Code _____